KEEPING THE FAITH

KEEPING THE FAITH

A Guide to the Christian Message

DAVID G. TRUEMPER
and
FREDERICK A. NIEDNER, JR.

FORTRESS PRESS   Philadelphia

Biblical quotations from the Revised Standard Version of the Bible, copyrighted 1946, 1952, © 1971, 1973 by the Division of Christian Education of the National Council of the Churches of Christ in the U.S.A., are used by permission.

The quotation at p. 30 is taken from *J. B.*, by Archibald MacLeish. Copyright © 1956, 1957, 1958 by Archibald MacLeish. Reprinted by permission of the publisher, Houghton Mifflin Company.

COPYRIGHT © 1981 BY FORTRESS PRESS

All rights reserved. No part of this publication may be reproduced, stored in a retrieval system, or transmitted in any form or by any means, electronic, mechanical, photocopying, recording, or otherwise, without the prior permission of the copyright owner.

Second printing 1983

Library of Congress Cataloging in Publication Data

Truemper, David G.
  Keeping the faith.

  1. Theology, Doctrinal—Popular works. 2. Lutheran Church—Doctrinal and controversial works. I. Niedner, Frederick A., 1945- II. Title.
BT77.T77   230'.41   81-43072
ISBN 0-8006-1608-1   AACR2

563G83   Printed in the United States of America   1-1608

To our parents
George and Erna Truemper,
Frederick and Esther Niedner,
keepers of the faith

CONTENTS

Introduction   9

1. Doctrine: Keeping the Good News Good   13

2. God: Moving Beyond Speculation to Trust   23

3. Justice and Mercy: Getting God's Creatures Loved in Spite of It All   35

4. The Gospel: God, in Jesus, Suffers Justly, for Mercy's Sake   53

5. Christology: Getting the Story Straight and the Promise Trustable   63

6. Faith: Trusting the Promise and Getting in on the Story   79

7. The Church: Spirited People Keeping the Story Alive and Keeping Alive by the Story   88

8. Christian Prayer: Words for the Struggle to Live by the Spirit — 100

9. Baptism: Born of the Spirit of Christ into Abba's Family — 117

10. Confession and Absolution: Keeping Peace in the Family and Keeping the Family in One Piece — 126

11. Holy Communion: Taking Part in the Fame and the Fate of Jesus — 134

INTRODUCTION

Keeping the Faith is a brief summary of, and guide to, Christian teachings. It is written with a conscious attempt to avoid the trappings of professional theology. It is frankly intended for amateurs —remembering, of course, that an amateur is one who loves something and engages in that activity not for profit but for love. We think there are hosts of amateur theologians in the churches, people who are serious about the business of thinking out loud about their faith but who do not gain their livelihood as professors, teachers, pastors, and the like. The book is also intended for people who are not yet amateurs but who are at least ready to listen to what the faith is all about—and who might well join the ranks of the theological amateurs.

Keeping means, naturally, holding on to, preserving, guarding. We hope we've done that in this book. It is a very *traditional* summary of Christian doctrine, talking about God and sin and Christ and salvation and faith and the church and prayer and the sacraments. It takes the biblical witness with utter seriousness, for that biblical witness to the Christian message is our unique access to the events of the life of Israel and of Jesus. It takes with full seriousness, also, the tradition of the church and its teaching. We place no premium on innovation in the stuff of doctrine, even though we have sought to present that stuff in a manner that is decidedly contemporary, with the help of images that are, we hope, rather fresh and, we admit, occasionally *untraditional*.

But *keeping* also means *tending*, caring for, nurturing—as of bees or sheep or zoological specimens. The faith is for keeping and tending. Doctrine is what the church does to tend the faith, to keep it alive and well and living in its people. This book is an attempt to offer help for just that purpose. It aims to help Christians in their work of tending the faith they hold, nurturing their understanding of it precisely for the changes and chances of this present age. We therefore attempt to interpret Christian doctrine not as the sum total of the assertions and propositions which Christian people hold dear but as instruction to the bearers of the Christian message about *how* to bear that message well, *how* to tell their story in such a way that Christ is glorified and sinners hear the good news. The terms *doctrine* and *teachings* are used interchangeably to refer to what Christians regard as the necessary parts of the church's message.

The advanced amateur theologian will quickly notice the book's pedigree. It is, rather unashamedly, a kind of catechism, or at least a commentary on the catechism. Catechism, of course, is a word that has been around in the church almost since the very beginning. It is the name for the manual of instruction in the faith used to prepare newcomers to the church for their baptism and incorporation into the church. But of course, one never outgrows one's need for the catechism; one needs continually to pray and meditate one's way through the basics of the faith. And so the catechism has been an important resource to Christians of all levels of maturity over the centuries.

The particular catechetical tradition out of which this book comes is that of the Lutheran reformation. The six chief parts of the catechisms of Luther are only thinly veiled in the chapters that follow. Yet to stand in the Lutheran tradition (at its best, at least) means something more than the furtherance of a particular party line. The faith confessed by the first-generation "Lutherans" at

Augsburg in 1530 was understed to be the *common* Christian faith, confessed in a way which sought to defend that faith against certain abuses in the life and piety of the late medieval European church. In that sense, then, this is a Lutheran book—it is an attempt to teach the *common* Christian faith, not a few precious slogans. Lutherans, like others, aim to help keep the church in the *common* Christian faith.

As a catechism-oriented book, *Keeping the Faith* does not cover the entire range of Christian doctrine, nor does it offer a thorough survey of even the major points of doctrine. Its themes are dictated by the catechetical tradition in which it stands, and, as a result, it does not take up other topics such as theological anthropology, ethics, or eschatology. Should some very advanced amateur theologian happen across this book, he or she would soon notice that the book is not a systematic theology, not even a little one. Naturally, many of the topics which we treat only briefly could be made the subject of book-length discussions in their own right. Our goal, however, is not exhaustive completeness but a handy treatment of the basics—a manual by which the doctrinal work of the church is accounted for and, we hope, furthered.

A recurring motif in this book is that of *story*. We understand the Christian message to be a story about Israel and about Jesus, a story which needs to be told well if its distinctive element is to be caught by its hearers. That distinctive element is what Christians call the "gospel," the good news that this Jesus-story really amounts to God's promise to be merciful and forgiving to the sinners whom Jesus befriended. The story of the friend of sinners, when rightly told, conveys the promise that modern hearers can also get in on the story and find themselves befriended and forgiven and enlivened by the God whom Jesus called "Abba," Daddy. We have not consciously attempted to take a position in the significant contemporary discussion of "narrative theology" and its virtues and limitations. We simply recognize that story has been a fundamental part of biblical thought, at least since the Israelites first kept the Passover meal as a remembrance of God's deliverance at the Sea of Reeds; they told the story of their miraculous deliverance, and thereby they understood themselves to be partakers in those events. That's what a well-told story does. And our manual is an attempt to help the Christian storytellers to do their job well, amateurs and almost-amateurs alike, and maybe even a professional here or there.

The authors come at their task out of their careers as teachers of undergraduates at a private, self-consciously Christian university. Each has also served a brief stint as a seminary professor. Each has been actively involved in the ministry of the campus chapel, in connection with which he has engaged in catechetical preaching. The one is a biblical theologian, the other a systematician. The work in this volume is, as much as possible, the joint responsibility of the two authors. The format of the book was determined in common, and the shape of each of the chapters was developed in extensive discussion. Though one or the other author prepared the initial draft of any given chapter, both authors understand themselves fully and jointly responsible for what is said in the following pages.

Our frank hope is that the reader will find that this commentary on the Christian catechism has both kept the faith and assisted the reader in keeping the faith, as well.

Valparaiso, Indiana
The Week of Prayer for
Christian Unity, 1981

DAVID G. TRUEMPER
FREDERICK A. NIEDNER

1
DOCTRINE

Keeping the Good News Good

When Jesus carried out his ministry, he announced by his life and his words that the kingdom of God had arrived; he spoke and acted so as to show the kingdom's coming and to bring it about—especially by his crucifixion and resurrection. But he did not really leave a body of teaching behind him. Though he was known as a teacher, and indeed as a spectacularly authoritative teacher ("he taught them as one who had authority, and not as their scribes," Matt. 7:29), and though the gospels frequently use the word "teach" to describe Jesus' activity, he nevertheless did not really fit the mold of the initiator of new religious ideas or teachings. His legacy to his disciples was not a body of doctrines but the memory of his call to follow and of his death "for our salvation."

How, then, did it become possible and even necessary to develop a body of doctrine, or a summary of the teachings, of the Christian church? To be sure, some have argued that the very existence of the church and of its teachings is already a serious and fatal departure from the vitality of the ministry of Jesus. Jesus came preaching the kingdom of God, and what resulted was only the church—so goes one of the put-downs. Others, including ourselves, are hardly so pessimistic about the development of doctrine in the church. Part of the aim of this chapter is to account for that development by showing the continuity between Jesus' announcement of the kingdom of God and his redemptive death, on the one hand, and the body of doctrine or teaching which we call the Christian faith, on the other. We shall do so not in order to claim some unique authority for the particular summary of Christian doctrine given here. We simply want to show that the central concern of the body of Christian teaching is the same as the central concern of the apostles, whose writings in the New Testament constitute the earliest, authoritatively unique witness to the meaning of the life and death of Jesus.

To put it as directly as possible: *Doctrine is what a Christian has to say in order that what gets heard will be the gospel.* Doctrine is instruction to Christian spokespersons, whether neophytes or veterans, amateurs or professionals, on how to speak about Jesus in such a way that the people who hear what they say will hear nothing less than the gospel—the good news about Jesus crucified and risen for their life and salvation. The main job of the body of Christian teaching, then, is to keep clear the confession about Jesus; that is, to keep that confession coming across as the good news its first confessors had heard. As we shall see, doctrine is thus aimed in several directions, to fulfill that same task for different groups of people and in several different situations.

First, as a summary of the Christian faith, doctrine has served to instruct newcomers to the church about the breadth and depth of their newfound faith. In early centuries, this instruction or catechesis usually took place during the period of Lent, in preparation for the catechumens' baptism at the Vigil of Easter, and it sometimes continued after the Easter baptisms until Pentecost in a series of additional sessions of teaching about the sacraments and the worship of the church. For new converts to the faith, doctrine served as a handy summary of what the Christian faith was all about—from sin's consequences, through Jesus' person and work, to the need for repentance and a holy life. A body of doctrine thus helped people who had come to hear the word about Jesus as good news to get past merely enjoying the warm glow about Jesus and to begin to understand not only the meaning of the faith but also the whole of their life and situation from the perspective of the Christian gospel.

Second, the church's doctrinal statements have also served as instructions to those charged with preaching, teaching, and evangelizing. "In order to say it right, say it this way"—such was the instruction given by the church's doctrine. After all, all sorts of things can be said about Jesus, and they usually were. It is possible, in fact, so to talk about Jesus that there is no good news at all. That sort of thing had happened already in the very earliest stage of the church's life, already during Jesus' lifetime. The crowds are reported to have been enthusiastic about Jesus, whether after a miraculous healing or after a bout with the scribes and Pharisees; yet the gospels repeatedly suggest that Jesus was not endorsing such enthusiasm, for "the Son of man must suffer many things" (Mark 8:31), and only so would his mission be understood properly. Therefore, it became important also after Jesus' death and resurrection to ensure that those who bore the message of the gospel did so rightly.

Such was, in fact, the situation in Galatia to which St. Paul addressed an epistle. After his missionary activity there, others came preaching another gospel (Gal. 1:6–7) which really was no gospel, no good news, at all, since it talked about Jesus in a way which left him to have died in vain, a way which did not provide consolation and hope but only more demand and more accusation. One way, then, to understand what Paul was aiming for in the Galatian letter is to see him offering instruction on how to talk about Jesus rightly, so as not to waste his dying and so as not to leave people without comfort. In this sense, doctrine is instruction to speakers of the Christian message on how to say it so that people hear good news.

Related to the previous situation is the third area in which the church's developing doctrinal tradition aimed to serve a useful purpose. Careful doctrinal formulations came to be made in order to deal with erroneous and contrary teaching, whether in the name of Christ or of some other claimant to people's faith and worship.

In fact, some histories of the early church are written as the story of the progressive definition of key doctrines over against the alien teachings of other popular religions of the time, and of Christian heretics (like Arius or Nestorius or Paul of Samosata). Not that, but this—such was the implied form of doctrinal statements, for every doctrinal assertion rules out some antithetical formulation.

When Arius sought to say that Jesus was not God like God but a creature of God and therefore subordinate to the Father, the consensus of the bishops of the church emerged in key statements that we now know as the Nicene Creed: "God from God, Light from Light, true God from true God, begotten, not made, of one Being with the Father." These more elaborate statements about the person of Jesus are not made out of a merely theoretical interest in ascribing nice and important things to a religious hero. They are said in order to keep clear a gospel which meets the same two criteria that we saw Paul appealing to in the Galatian letter; that is, a gospel which does not waste the death of Jesus and which does not fail to offer godly consolation and hope to sinners. This use of doctrine aims to rule out that sort of error which would fail to be really good news to sinners.

We have so far sketched three kinds of situations in the life of the church in which the development of doctrinal statements and definitions played an important and necessary role. It should be clear by now that the church's teaching is *not* to be seen as a body of pet ideas and notions, the believing of which makes one a member of the church. Rather, doctrine ought to be useful, as instruction to neophytes and to official and unofficial spokespersons for the Christian message, on what sorts of things need to be said so that what gets heard will be in fact the Christian gospel and not something less good than that ultimately good news. In what follows, we shall amplify these notions and sketch some additional concerns: the relationship between doctrine and the Scriptures, the connection of doctrine with the cultural and historical situation of the church, the difference between doctrine and gospel, and the fact that the development of doctrinal statements is the church's work of keeping its witness faithful to its origins yet communicable in new situations.

Doctrine and Scripture

Christian doctrine offers a surprising solution to the problem of human existence under the domination of sin and death—the crucified Jesus. It is the same solution which the Bible offers, with its message of God's justice and mercy. Thus, we are at the core of both the biblical and doctrinal tasks when we describe these tasks as diagnosing the human condition in order to offer as good news to that condition the gospel about God's mercy and forgiveness on account of Jesus.

We are not far from the truth when we say that the Bible is problem-solving literature. The word that Jesus himself preached was of that sort, as he sought to expose the legalism and works-oriented religion of his day and as he proclaimed to sinners and religious leaders alike the readiness of God to act graciously, to forgive, and to give life and healing to his people. The New Testament writers sought to make a similar diagnosis of the situation of the primitive church, in order to offer the same good news in that new situation. Thus, for example, Paul sought to show the Galatian Christians that the different gospel to which they had succumbed was not just an alien teaching (in which case Paul would simply have been personally miffed that they had replaced their allegiance to his ideology with allegiance to a different set of teachings). It was far worse, for it left its adherents caught in the same old web of sin and death, of *law* and *flesh* (to use key terms from the Galatian letter). The problem in which the Galatians found themselves was as bad as it could be; they were locked in a no-win situation where their rightness before God depended on their ability to produce perfect obedience to all the details of the law, a situation in which the only possible result was death to the sinners. The good news for that bad situation was that God aims to deal mercifully, not retributively, with sinners— even with Galatian sinners. God had dealt according to promise already with Abraham, Paul reminded his readers, and now, "in Christ Jesus you are all sons of God, through faith. For as many of you as were baptized into Christ have put on Christ" (Gal. 3:26–27). And promises, as we shall see in a later chapter, can be received only by trusting them!

Similarly, Christian doctrine is a problem-solving process—but in the new situation in which the post-New Testament church finds itself. When Jesus is no longer on the scene, and when the apostles are no longer around, and when the church is no longer living within the Jewish community but out in the Gentile world of different political systems and alien philosophical systems and the mystery religions—*how*, then, shall the message of Jesus be stated, and *how* shall the church order its life, and *how* shall one tell whether this or that teacher of the faith is speaking the truth? As the years went by, Christian doctrine developed as a summary of those essential matters which, if lost or mutilated or twisted, would fail to carry out adequately the problem-solving mission of the Christian message. At the same time, however, those doctrinal formulations were subjected to the authority of Scripture. That is, the church sought to have its teaching of the faith conformed to the authentic problem-solving message of the Scriptures in the fresh situations in which it found itself. Thus, precisely in order to say the same old thing, the saving message about the forgiving mercy of God, the church found it necessary to say new things, to develop new formulations, to find new vocabulary, and to make use of new language and symbols. The development of doctrine is the process by which that was accomplished.

Throughout the church's history, there have been diverse approaches to the interpretation of this authoritative scripture. Some of these approaches have been mutually contradictory. It is even possible to write the history of the church's theology as the history of the interpretation of the Scriptures. A thorough discussion of the problems posed by this diversity in interpretation is beyond the scope of the present book, but it is probably useful to offer a few comments on the approach taken, at least implicitly, by this book's authors.

Standing in the tradition of the Lutheran reformation, we follow two crucial principles. First, the Bible is open to the application of all the tools and skills of human interpretative effort (including the linguistic and humanistic tools of Renaissance scholarship, as well as most of the other techniques developed by scholars since that time). Accordingly, there is no unique or distinctive set of principles for the proper interpretation of the biblical text. Second, the essential element in biblical interpretation is to discern how a given text relates to, aids, or enables the communication of the criticism and comfort which the word of God offers to the human situation. Accordingly, we will regularly move beyond mere literary or historical judgments about the biblical text to their theological (i.e., gospel-oriented) meaning. At times we may seem relatively unconcerned about historical detail or about the accuracy of this or that image or literary device used by the biblical writers, in order to make a theological observation or to derive a gospel-oriented conclusion from our reference to the Scriptures.

It is wise at this point to remember that the notion of a canon of sacred writings developed parallel to the creation of specific doctrinal formulations. *Canon* means measuring-stick, ruler, or straightedge. Used about the Bible, canon means the list of approved books—approved in the sense that the church recognized the message of these books, and just these books, to be uniquely and accurately the authentic message of the apostles and prophets, and therefore the unique standard for the message and worship of the church in subsequent centuries. There were other gospel-books, other letters claiming apostolic authorship, and other apocalypses as well, but the early church gradually received and acknowledged a particular list as authentically apostolic. And the church's spokespersons were expected to conform their proclamation and teaching to the standards contained in those books.

Doctrine and Situation

It would be misleading only to say that in the development of doctrine the church sought to remain faithful to the authentic apostolic witness to the gospel that is found in the Bible. Another factor played into the process of doctrinal development as well. After all, since doctrine is what must be said so that what people hear will be the gospel, it should be evident that doctrine is responsibly related not only to the biblical sources but also to the historical and cultural situation in which the church finds itself at a given juncture.

Some dimensions of that cultural connectedness are especially evident. You cannot talk in Latin or Swahili if you want people to hear the gospel in Des Moines, Iowa. You'll need to speak American English—and probably with a midwestern twang to your voice, as well, since midwesterners are notoriously suspicious of people who speak with a Boston accent, and Bostonians respond in kind. But the very fact that the gospel is a problem-solving message requires also more subtle forms of cultural conditioning. The Iowans in Des Moines are not living in the same world of thought and culture as the citizens of Renaissance Florence—or of colonial Williamsburg, for that matter. Their values, their education, and their recreation are markedly different. So is the way in which they experience the bind of sin and death. And any Christian spokesperson had better walk a few miles in their shoes, so to speak, if his or her message is going to be heard as gospel there, or anywhere else, for that matter.

That is what we mean when we say that doctrine relates not only to the authoritative apostolic witness of the Bible but also to the historical and cultural situation of the church at a given time and place. For that reason, the church's doctrinal work is never done. In fact, saying the same old thing will frequently produce a message that either is not understood at all or is understood wrongly or in a distorted way.

Summaries of Christian doctrine are therefore notoriously short-lived. Their usefulness is limited by place and time, and by the cultural and historical situation for which they were initially created and in which they almost inevitably took the particular shape and tone which characterized them. The present summary is no exception. It frankly reflects the language and moods of the times, sometimes in ways that are not a part of the author's consciousness. But these will be evident, should by some miracle a copy of this volume survive for a century and be picked up by a survivor of the galactic wars of A.D. 2069.

Doctrine and Gospel

The decisive connection of the church's doctrine is not, however, with the Bible or with the cultural situation, important as those lines of connection are. The decisive connection is with the gospel for the sake of which doctrinal formulations have their entire reason for being. *Doctrine is saying what has to be there if gospel is going to be heard.* This leads to a double connection between doctrine and gospel.

On the one hand, doctrine is what exists for the sake of the gospel, so that the gospel can be heard and trusted and celebrated in ever new situations. Doctrine is then the stockroom, the storehouse, of what the church needs in order to carry out its work. Here doctrine is what the church says to itself so that it has gospel to say to those who need to hear it (whether those hearers are already inside the church or still on the outside). What we are saying is simply that doctrine is the church's homework, done to ensure the authenticity of its gospel.

On the other hand, however, there is a sense in which doctrine really is the same as the gospel. Precisely because of its intimate connection with the good news, doctrine takes on the characteristics of that good news. The church forms its doctrinal statements in such a way that they actually convey the gospel; doctrinal statements are thus exemplary ways of saying the gospel. As we said earlier, doctrine consists of instructions to Christian spokespersons on how to say the message so that what gets heard is really the Christian good news.

Christian doctrine is thus a particular form of gospel statement, designed to set the pattern of how the gospel is to be said and done. This is surely the case when we view doctrinal statements as instructions to official spokespersons, but it is also true for the work of teaching the faith to neophytes or ordinary Christian people. Here is what the Christian faith is all about, the church would say. Here is how the faith hangs together and hooks up with the situation in which you find yourself. Here is a way to think about the faith so as to catch its implications for your own believing and living. And above all, here is a way to learn rightly to praise a God who promises forgiveness and life and salvation to those who come to trust the promises that are indeed good news.

2
GOD

Moving Beyond Speculation to Trust

Basic to the study of Christian doctrine is the assumption that there is a God, some being who is in control of the universe and who is in some sense responsible for its existence. As necessary and as natural as that assumption might appear to be, it is not so easily made today as it once was, and it therefore requires discussion.

We moderns have been conditioned to think of the world as though there were no God, or at least as though God's existence were unnecessary and thus as though the question of God's existence were meaningless. For example, very few people today would assume that the weather is in any direct sense the work of a God who controls such things. We all know that the atmospheric conditions are caused by the interactions of high and low pressure systems, humidity levels, and other natural factors, which we may monitor quite carefully with the help of satellite photographs and television weather forecasters. When we become ill, we do not immediately assume the condition to be the work of God. We know all too well of the effects of viruses, bacteria, carcinogens, and cholesterol upon our bodies. Seeds germinate, human beings reproduce, and the planets continue to circle the sun, all without the apparent need for assistance or control by some deity. The assumption of God's existence has become unnecessary and even meaningless in our day-to-day existence, and serious talk about God has been relegated to such special circumstances as churchly gatherings or moments of extreme fear.

The Problem of God-Talk in a Secular Age

We are the children of a secular culture. *Secularism* is the name given to a style of life and thought which is based upon the assumption that the meaning of things may be discussed and decisions may be made without reference to a deity. To some extent, our growing awareness of the natural causes of events and circumstances has generated secularism, but secularism has also resulted from the influence of certain formal systems of thought.

Perhaps the most important among those philosophies is one which goes by the name *positivism*. Positivism is a kind of thinking which assumes that anything which is transcendent, that is, totally different from us and outside the normal range of experience, cannot be meaningfully discussed. Thus, because the existence of a transcendent deity cannot be proved or disproved, at least not on the basis of experience, its existence makes no difference and it is meaningless to talk about it.

That assumption as it has been applied to God is illustrated rather clearly in the so-called "Parable of the Invisible Gardener." In the parable, two men are walking through a forest and come upon a clearing in the trees. One of the men states that he believes a gardener has taken care of that clearing. The other man asks for evidence to that effect and points out that this clearing is like all the other clearings in the forest. The work of a gardener was not apparent in the design of the clearing. The first man concedes this point but persists in his opinion. The skeptic then suggests that they wait until the gardener should appear, since that would settle the argument. They wait an entire year. In that time no gardener comes, but the clearing springs up with foliage almost exactly as it had the year before. This prompts the first man to insist that the gardener is invisible and has in fact come but has been undetected by the two men. The skeptic then installs every conceivable detection device around the clearing, and still another year goes by without any gardener being detected in the area, while the clearing grows the same as always. The first man continues to believe that an invisible gardener tends the clearing. But the skeptic, who is the positivist in the parable, maintains that while it is possible that there is such a gardener, a gardener's presence makes no difference and therefore is foolish even to discuss.

What cannot be verified or falsified by experience makes no difference. Such is the verdict of positivism upon the idea of a transcendent God responsible for the control and origin of the world. Those who wish may believe there is such a being, but it is nonsense to speak of it because it changes nothing. It is simply talk.

The difficulty which this line of thought poses for traditional Christianity is obvious. While it can hardly be doubted that some two thousand years ago there lived a man named Jesus of Nazareth, the traditional belief that this person somehow was or represented a transcendent deity, a creator, becomes nonsense in the minds of those trained to think in a secular way.

In recent years, however, several new modes of theological thinking have been developed in an attempt to circumvent the secular critique of traditional conceptions of a transcendent God. *Process theology*, for example, is an attempt to reformulate the ancient ideas of pantheism (everything is God) and panentheism (God is in everything). Its value in the confrontation with secular thought is that it removes God from the realm of transcendence and makes God a part of everyday experience. God either is, or is in, everything.

The problem is still not easily solved, however, even by process theology. Strictly pantheistic forms of process thought offer a solution which is merely semantic. Everything is still everything, just as always, but now we have agreed to call it "God." Nothing has really changed except the name. Panentheistic forms of process thought offer more help. God can be said to be a part of common experience and to endure precisely what humanity endures. Yet because in this kind of thought God is still finally something to some extent different from the world and outside human experience, the problems of transcendence remain.

A Secular View of the World

A more substantive response to the secular challenge inherent in our culture and in ourselves may be to admit that logically it makes as much sense to say that there is no transcendent God as to say that there is. By the canons of logic, both statements may be successfully defended, and at least logically, therefore, the possibility exists that Christian theology as well as all other attempted talk about God is an exercise in nonsense.

It is worth noting at this point that in some respects the secular world is a rather stark place. If the universe is not the work of a creator, it is an accident. It is a rather grand and marvelous accident but an accident nonetheless. The same might be said of every human being. Furthermore, people and things have no ultimate objective value, only a subjective value. I may not wish for a murderer to kill me, and my family and friends might join in that wish because they value my life, but ultimately it makes no difference whether the murderer kills me or not, because my life is only an accident in the first place. It has no ultimate, objective value to anyone except myself. By extension, even the mass slaughter of Armenians, Jews, or Cambodians cannot be evaluated ultimately in an accidental world because there is no ultimate value placed upon the slaughtered by anyone but themselves. It was neither right nor wrong to have killed so many, from this point of view. It simply happened.

In defense of the morality of most practicing secular people, it is only fair to say that they do operate with systems of value and distinguish right from wrong. Such value systems, however, are grounded only in the mutual consent of those who agree to operate with the same or similar evaluations of property, life, and the behavior which affects either or both.

Nevertheless, very few people today would be willing to agree that genocide such as the world has witnessed three different times in this century is neither right nor wrong, and that genocide is to be evaluated only in terms of whether one finds oneself among the killers or the killed. Indeed, it is a virtually universal assumption today that what Hitler did to the Jews was horribly and intrinsically wrong. Thus, even though the world can function today without the need for belief in a transcendent deity, men and women still assume almost universally that there are values, especially related to such things as life itself, which transcend private values and even the values of common consent which vary from culture to culture. Since there is no value apart from evaluation, to assume transcendent value implies the assumption, even if only at an unconscious level, that there is some ultimate external evaluator or evaluative standard.

Arguments for the Existence of God

The importance of that common assumption in the present discussion is that it represents the basis of one of the oldest of all arguments for the existence of God. Writers as different in their perspectives as Aristotle, St. Paul, St. Thomas Aquinas, and a number of modern philosophers have argued that the universal assumption of transcendent evaluation implies the existence of an ultimate evaluator, to whose evaluation one may finally appeal and in whose evaluation one has ultimate value. Such an evaluator, said Thomas in the thirteenth century, is commonly called *God*. At this point we are not yet talking about a personal deity or even a creator but merely an impersonal evaluator or judge.

The problem of values in a secular culture such as ours has been discussed first, because it exposes the most obvious weakness in the system of assumptions upon which secularism is based. The argument for the existence of transcendent evaluation, sometimes known as the *moral argument* for the existence of God, is therefore the logical one with which to begin stating the case which can be made for God's existence. There are other arguments, and the most important of those are rehearsed below. It is currently fashionable among philosophers to offer such arguments once again, but the recent discussions have really been little more than variations on the work of Thomas, who in turn was applying the thought of Aristotle to Christian theology.

Thomas offered four other arguments in addition to the moral argument. First, he argued that everything which happens or exists in the world has been caused by something or someone, and therefore the world itself may be assumed to have been caused by some transcendent force of causation. He called this force the *uncaused first cause* and noted that most people call it *God*. Second, Thomas observed that the whole world is in a constant state of change but that the recognition of change implies the existence of something stable against which change may be gauged, or, as he called it, an *unmoved prime mover*, that most refer to as *God*. Third, everything which happens or comes to be in the universe is contingent upon a vast array of prior circumstances or contingencies. The recognition of contingency, however, requires that at some point beyond all contingencies there exists something uncontingent, something *necessary in itself*, something most people call *God*. Finally, Thomas argued that the world cannot have been an accident but must be the product of an intelligent force because of its intricate design and harmonious functioning. Such intricacy and harmony could only be the work of an intelligent creator, whom most refer to as *God*.

Thomas's arguments must be understood as arguments, not as proofs, and he himself noted that in each case an alternative argument could be lodged. It could be that value is only imaginary, that the chains of causation, change, and contingency are in fact infinite and that there is no uncaused, unchanged, or necessary force responsible for the universe. The universe may indeed be accidental, unnecessary, and fundamentally expendable. And modern people, obviously, have no difficulty in imagining the harmony of nature and the intricacy of its design as the products of long eons of natural selection of species which are fittest and most adaptable to conditions. Nevertheless, Thomas's arguments and the modern variations on them suggest that it is just as probable that there is a God as it is that there is not. The odds appear to be even.

Christian faith and theology both clearly assume that there is a God, and from this point on in our discussion we will operate with that assumption. It is always worth remembering, however, the ways by which we have arrived at our assumptions and that there are alternatives to them.

The God of Human Speculation

What exactly is gained by assuming that the world is no accident but the product of a designer, a necessary agent of causation, and an evaluator? The answer to that may lie in the assumption that the world is the product of someone's will. Someone wanted a world. The universe is the product of wish or desire, as is everything and everyone in it, at least to some degree. This assumption, in turn, establishes the ultimate, inherent value of the world and the creatures within it. The creator desired to make and to have the creature. The creature is the creator's bright idea, an object of desire and therefore of value.

But that is only half of the evaluating which our assumptions imply. If all creatures are objects of desire and therefore of value, then the interaction between the various creatures must also be evaluated. One creature who damages or destroys another creature has destroyed something which is not a useless, accidental phenomenon but the object of the creator's desire. Moreover, if all creatures have value, all interactions among creatures must be evaluated in terms of their effect upon all other objects of the creator's desire. Thus, our assumptions about God gain for us an inherent value as individuals, but they also mean that *we* are being evaluated. When we harm other creatures, or even ourselves, we become the opponents of the creator whose bright ideas all creatures are. Our assumptions have led, it seems, directly into difficulty.

The difficulty only begins there. We confront additional problems when we ponder the relationship of God as the creator of the objects of his desire and God as the first cause upon whom all subsequent causes and effects depend. The problem arises specifically when we consider the existence of *evil* in the creation.

On the basis of the evidence available to us in the creation, we may characterize the creator as powerful, clever, and at least to some degree favorably disposed to the creatures. The magnitude and intricacy of the universe, from galaxies to chromosomes, and the beauty of both nature and human experience would suggest this. However, the same first cause must be responsible for both ants and anteaters, for the cells of brain tumors as well as the human brain, for volcanoes as well as for the people whom these incinerate. It is one thing to ponder war, which may be explained as the result of distorted values among the creatures, who in some way share the capacity to will or desire and to cause certain events. It is another matter when the cause of evil cannot be traced to human origin. What kind of creator or first cause would be responsible for the death of a million Chinese in an earthquake, or even the death of a single child with leukemia? As Nickles, a character in Archibald MacLeish's play *J. B.* (Boston: Houghton Mifflin, 1956, p. 11), said, "If God is God He is not good; if God is good He is not God." Either God's goodness or God's omnipotence must be questioned in the face of evil.

At best, the evidence available in nature suggests that the creator or first cause is rather capricious, one moment giving life and the next snuffing it out in whimsical fashion, or so it seems to us. Indeed, the suffering which attends so many deaths by natural causes makes the first cause appear worse than whimsical. The creator seems to lack mercy.

The *problem of evil and its origins* is vexing and perplexing. Few theological and philosophical problems have made agnostics of as many people as has the problem of evil. Traditionally, Christians have spoken to this problem in three basic ways. First, if God is assumed to be totally good, then the existence of evil is inexplicable. It is simply one of the many kinds of mysteries. Second, evil has been blamed upon freedom. God, in this line of thought, neither coerces people nor operates them as puppets. As a result, human freedom is used (or abused) for the perpetration of evil. There are problems with this view, of course, since it is still God who allows freedom, and the freedom must be extended to inanimate objects in order to explain natural disasters. Killer earthquakes, for example, are viewed simply as free sections of the earth's freely cooling surface, which in their movements accidentally kill free human beings who happen to be living above those sections.

Third, there is a more specifically Christian approach. It begins with the observation that Christianity has no independent theory on the origin of evil, since all of the images used in the Bible to explain the source of evil come from non-Israelite or non-Christian sources. Christians have focused instead upon what they regard as God's response to evil, namely, the cross of Christ. Finally, regardless of its origin, evil is overcome by God's own submission to the evil that works ruin and terror in the creation.

The great mystery, then, is not so much the origin of evil as the source and existence of goodness, love, and mercy. That is quite consistently the biblical viewpoint. The Old Testament does not even treat the problem of evil's origins in a direct way in its earlier writings. What is described instead is the remarkable fact of God's mercy for evil's perpetrators and victims, mercy which is to be worked out through Abraham and his descendants.

Only the latest Old Testament documents introduce the figure of Satan (see Job 1–2; Zech. 3:1–2; 1 Chron. 21:1), and even there Satan is not described as a supernatural being who is responsible for evil. Rather, Satan is a kind of tempter or prosecuting attorney in the cosmic judgment hall. In any case, Satan is introduced from the literature of Persia and related cultures neighboring Israel in postexilic times. The New Testament writers, especially in books such as Revelation, are dependent upon the post-Old Testament development sometimes called *dualism*, the assumption that an infinitely good force (God) is locked in perpetual combat with an infinitely evil force (Satan or the Evil One), with humankind as the pawn and booty in the struggle.

Were we to ask the scriptural sources alone to answer the question of the origins of evil, they would trace it to the human heart. The desire of people to be something more than human is what first unleashes evil (see Gen. 3:1–7). It is over the human heart as the source of evil that Yahweh, the creator, despairs both before and after the flood (Gen. 6:5–8 and 8:20–21), and Jesus traces the problem to the identical source (Mark 7:20–23). That source of evil will be considered later in the discussion of *the flesh* (see chapter 8), as Paul and others designated the drive for self-preservation at any cost and regardless of the effect upon others. While it is true that evil becomes institutionalized, and the whole of it in such situations as wars, ghettos, and racism is greater than the sum of its parts (i.e., individual human hearts), to blame that evil upon some outside force like the devil or Satan is to excuse oneself too easily and to ignore the real source of evil, the New Testament suggests. And if the self-preserving human heart is the source of evil, then the real mystery is why someone would lay down his life for his friends and why in his name others would do likewise.

What we have described up to this point is the *God of human speculation*, the deity whose nature and character may be extrapolated from the preceding assumptions and from the evidence available in nature as the product of that deity's will or desire. The *God of human speculation* is clever and powerful and an ultimate evaluator of human life and behavior, but also at least to some extent capricious and pitiless. There is no unambiguous evidence or logic by which we may assume that this God is personally and permanently interested in any individual creature, or that there is anything but simple justice for those who interact improperly with others among the creator's bright ideas.

The God of Abraham and Jesus

At the foundation of the faith and theology of the Judeo-Christian tradition is the belief that the creator is both just and loving, the ultimate evaluator but also totally merciful. As we have seen above, the justice and evaluation ascribed to God in Christian theology may be deduced, at least in primitive form, from nature. The love and mercy of that God, however, remain hidden from the creation, and in the perspective of the Judeo-Christian tradition are revealed only in the personal relationship which God established with Abraham and Sarah, Isaac and Rebekah, and Jacob and his family, and which Christians believe is fulfilled in the person of Jesus Christ.

Even in the presence of Abraham, Sarah, or Jesus of Nazareth, the love of God may remain hidden from an observer. Not everyone who knew them saw in them any evidence that God is gracious. But those who observed their lives from the perspective of faith saw in them the evidence that God is not only just but an incurable lover. God chooses and blesses Israel and remains faithful to the people despite their lack of trust in God. Moreover, the reason why they are chosen at all is that this God might bring the blessing of mercy to the lives of all the families of the earth. Curse, judgment, punishment, and death have been the consequences of the creatures' improper interactions with one another. Such has been the creator's evaluation and justice, but now God becomes involved intimately in the lives of a people in order that ultimately all creatures might come to know God's love and compassion for them.

At the heart of the Christian gospel is the belief that in Jesus of Nazareth the creator has taken on the flesh and blood of the creature in the ultimate act of compassion. In this one man, God exhibits mercy and endures the judgment of God's own evaluation. In Jesus, God dies as any other creature must, under the terms of God's evaluation. In this Jesus Christ, then, is the ultimate truth about God: God is ultimately both just and loving. The surest consequence of being both judge and lover of the same creature is, as the prophet Hosea so boldly and poignantly portrays (Hos. 11:8-9), suffering. One must execute one's own beloved and live with the resulting broken heart. If the God of Abraham and Sarah is the creator and first cause, and if Jesus Christ is God incarnate, then God is neither impersonal nor pitiless. God's heart is known in the story of Israel and of Jesus to be merciful and compassionate, even broken, for the sake of the creatures.

Conclusion

In the remainder of this discussion of Christian doctrine we will assume that this is the truth about the heart of God, and we will consistently assume as well that God's heart is hidden in Jesus Christ and revealed uniquely there. There is no heart of mercy in the *God of human speculation*. That heart is known only to those who are themselves in Christ and who look at themselves and the rest of creation from that perspective. That, at least, is the point of the Christian faith. In what follows we seek to give an accounting of the grounds for that assumption.

3
JUSTICE AND MERCY

Getting God's Creatures Loved in Spite of It All

From the perspective of those who are "in Christ," the creator's creation and the evaluator's system of evaluation appear differently than they do to the speculative thinker who knows only the impersonal first cause. One of the earliest of the doctrinal statements adopted by Christians reflects this difference. The Nicene Creed begins with a statement of belief in "one God, the Father, the Almighty, maker of heaven and earth, of all that is, seen and unseen." Similarly, the later Apostles' Creed begins, "I believe in God, the Father almighty, creator of heaven and earth." It is no accident that in both cases the creeds confess belief in a deity who is first of all Father, and only then do they mention the power and work of that deity. That is, in the Christian's perspective the omnipotence and the creative work of God are to be seen in light of God's parental love. To speak of God first as Father is to speak of God as the Father of Jesus Christ and therefore as the merciful and loving God who is revealed in Jesus Christ, whose heart is broken for all the children, and whose gracious will is accomplished in the life and death of Jesus.

This God is personal and trustworthy. Should we reverse the perspectives and view God as Father in light of his power and creation, we are again confronted with a God who cannot be trusted, because, although apparently almighty, such a God allows or even administers evil and suffering in a most capricious manner. Of course, as we have seen above, evil remains in the world of that God, but the Father-God suffers more than anyone as a result. Or to use another image from the Old Testament, God is our Mother, loving and nurturing and comforting her children, never able to forget the children who have sucked at her breast. "As one whom his mother comforts, so I will comfort you," says Mother-God (Isa. 66:13). God is ultimately for us, not against us. God is our friend.

The Creator as Lover

With this assumption, we may examine the universe and see in nature and especially in human beings the hand of a lover at work. The accounts of creation in Genesis and elsewhere (e.g., Prov. 8:22–36; Job 38–39) discuss the origins of the universe from this perspective. For example, Genesis 1 portrays God as pausing at the end of each day's creative work to pronounce the results of the day's work as *good* or *pleasing.* God is pleased, since what was desired or wished for is now in existence. In Genesis 2, the first thing Yahweh (which is the name of God here and in many other places in the Old Testament) does after making the man is to plant a garden. And the name of the garden is *Eden*, which means *place of delight* in Hebrew.

Thus, the creation is the place of God's delight, and it is meant to be the setting for humanity's delight as well. This is also the point of the Sabbath or day of rest which God celebrates at the conclusion of the work of creation. God takes time off not out of weariness but in order to enjoy the creation. It is pleasing to God. God's creatures are also good, and they, too, will take time to enjoy themselves, one another, and the whole delightful creation. And when men and women pause from their labors, they may enjoy, even as their own creator does, the work of their hands.

In both Genesis accounts, the creation of humankind is the climax of the story. There the evidence that the creator is a lover is most clearly presented. Men and women are created last in Genesis 1, and they are to be the crown of the creation and its rulers. They are special, different from the other living things. God says prior to their creation, "Let us make man in our image" (Gen. 1:26), and then God proceeds to make both male and female in God's own image (1:27). God does not merely call them into being, as with the earlier creatures. Instead, God takes care to make them in a unique way.

What does it mean to be made *in the image of God?* It does not mean, as some have argued, that God has a body after which human beings are modeled. Rather, Genesis 1 considers human beings to be like God in two ways. First, men and women will have dominion over the rest of creation. God will share authority with them (1:26). Second, and even more significantly, to be made in God's image is to have something of God's own life within one. This is the intent of the prohibition against murder in Genesis 9:5–6. Animals may be killed for food, but human beings shall not be killed because they are made in the image of God. The implication is that human life is unique, as is God's own life.

But what exactly is the unique character of that life which God and humanity share? Is it only the power to rule over the remainder of creation? One of the few places in the Old Testament where human life is defined as unique is in Psalm 8. There, too, the proximity of human life to God's own is described (Ps. 8:5a), and the result of that relationship is that humankind is put in charge of creation (8:6). But there is more. The psalmist says (8:5b) that the Lord has crowned him (humankind) with glory and honor.

This is a highly significant description for understanding the Old Testament's view of humanity. The Hebrew word for *honor* refers to the beauty or dignified appearance of human beings, but the word for *glory* points to something more complex. Literally, it means "heaviness," and it is something generally ascribed to the creator alone. And with what is the creator heavy? Although the glory of God, according to the Old Testament, is to be seen to some extent in God's authority and judgment over the universe, ultimately it is revealed in acts of salvation and rescue on behalf of God's people (see, e.g., Isa. 35:1-2; 40:5; 58:8; and especially Ps. 85:8-11).

God, it appears, is weighty with both judgment and redemption. God is just, and God is a lover. To say, then, that humanity shares in the *glory* and *image* of God is to say that the ultimate gift of the creator to humanity is the ability to be both just and loving.

Genesis 2 presents a similar understanding of the relationship of humankind to the creator, although it does so with different imagery. Yahweh forms the man (*adam* in Hebrew) from the dust of the ground (*adamah* in Hebrew), much as a potter would form a clay pot, and then Yahweh breathes into that clay thing and it becomes a living being (Gen. 2:7). Later, when Yahweh makes other animals, they, too, are formed from the ground and given life. But the creator does not breathe into them (Gen. 2:19). The man's life is unique, for Yahweh's own life and breath are in him (Gen. 6:3). In the view of Genesis 2, this results at first in loneliness for the man. He cannot share his life with the animals, so Yahweh gives him a mate, or helper, woman. These two, both with the breath of Yahweh in them, have a unique capacity, and we may discover the nature of that capacity by examining the concept of God's "breath" in the Old Testament.

The word *breath* in Genesis 2:7 is synonymous with the word for the *breath* or *Spirit* of God used elsewhere in the Old Testament to refer to the agent or force by which God works. By means of *Spirit* or *wind* (one and the same word in Hebrew), God causes events in nature (see Gen. 8:1 or Exod. 15:10), and even certain types of human behavior are ascribed to the work of the Spirit (Judg. 14:19; 1 Sam. 11:6). But more often the term is used to refer to the nature of human life, and more specifically to that within human nature which is shared with the creator who gives that Spirit. Because a person has the Spirit of God in oneself, one has a conscience which searches the soul (Prov. 20:27), and one is able to understand in ways other creatures cannot (Job 32:8; 33:4; 34:14-15). The Spirit, therefore, is what gives to humankind the critical capacity, which is shared with God.

But the Spirit has another function. It also gives to humanity the ability to love. God breathes the Spirit into a wasted, dead nation, which has become no more than a valley of dry bones (Ezek. 37:1–14), so that the people are once again alive to do God's work of blessing on the earth. To have the Spirit of God within one is to have a heart of flesh (Ezek. 36:26–27); that is, a vulnerable heart, a heart which can be broken, a heart capable of compassion, a heart like the creator's.

Thus, the images used in both Genesis 1 and 2, as different as the accounts are, suggest that in the view of the Old Testament the creation exists because of the sheer desire and delight of the creator and remains as the object of that desire and the occasion for God's delight. Furthermore, humanity shares in the unique life of the creator and is therefore set apart from other creatures. Like God, men and women have not only the understanding and critical capacity to do justice but also the ability to be compassionate and therefore to do mercy.

Justice and Mercy in the Commandments

In both the previous and present chapters, the concepts of *value*, *evaluation*, and *justice* have played a major role in the discussion. Reflection upon these subjects immediately brings to mind the question of the standards by which evaluating is to be done or justice worked among men and women. Human cultures have traditionally operated with a specific body of law as the standard by which justice is done, and the Judeo-Christian tradition is no exception.

The Scriptures contain vast amounts of legislation, all of which is presented as the *law of God*, but the core of it may be seen in what is commonly called the Ten Commandments or the Decalogue. These commandments contain a demand for loyalty and obedience to a single deity, and they prohibit such acts as murder, adultery, theft, or perjury. In many respects, there is nothing unusual about these commandments. An almost identical list of basic demands and prohibitions is evident in or assumed by law codes as varied as Hammurabi's Code and the United States

Constitution. Given the perspective of the biblical writer, however, even the law and its core in the commandments must be viewed as the measure and expression of the will of the God who is not only just but also loving.

Both Jesus and Moses taught that obedience to the law of God consists in loving God and in loving one's neighbor as oneself (see Lev. 19:17–18, 33–34; Deut. 6:5; Matt. 22:35–40; also Rom. 13:8–10). In the perspective of Genesis and Exodus, the Decalogue was given to the people whom God had chosen as agents for blessing on the earth. We may expect, therefore, that the law is ultimately intended to serve the same purpose as the election of God's people. Furthermore, it is interesting to note that in the Old Testament's portrayal, the law was not presented to Israel until after God had rescued the people, thereby exhibiting and acting upon a deep love for them. The God who commands at Sinai is the same God who has known for a long time the sufferings of Israel in Egypt (Exod. 3:7–8). This "knowing" is the Old Testament's way of saying that God is intimate with Israel and suffers whatever they suffer. Their joy as well as their pain are God's also. Moreover, the law of this just and compassionate God requires precisely what God's will is; namely, that all men and women be loved by one another with God's own love, a love which is the unique capacity of God's own Spirit breathed into every human creature.

When viewed from that perspective, the Ten Commandments do not function only as arbitrary and negative prohibitions against idolatry and injurious behavior. They are also positive, in that they require men and women to embody the loving care which God wills all creatures to know and to have. The following discussion of the commandments develops that perspective.

The First Table of Commandments

I. *You shall have no other gods.* In a very real sense, this is the fundamental commandment, for to comply with the subsequent commandments is also to obey this first command, and to violate any of the others is to break this one as well. The first commandment is more than a prohibition of the kind of polytheism often associated with various religious systems containing a pantheon. It is also more than a prohibition of syncretism, which is the blending of various religious systems. The command requires that a person respect the justice of God, return the love of God, and trust in God alone as the source of one's life, identity, and personal value. To look anywhere else for identity, value, and meaning is to have another god, and in the course of a lifetime there are many other places one is tempted to look. A nation, a career, a lover, even a three-bedroom home in the suburbs—each can become a god if it becomes the center of a person's life, around which all else is organized, and if it functions for someone as the ultimate source and symbol of that person's identity and individual value.

Why should God be so jealous of that position? The answer lies in the secret of God's nature as both just and loving. God wills that all men and women should be loved with God's unique love, and other gods simply cannot deliver that love. Careers and possessions cannot really give us the love, the identity, and the value which God wills for human creatures. These take more than they return. Even lovers cannot adequately serve as gods, because when they are expected to provide identity, value and a reason to live, God's kind of loving is not being done. It is actually one's own welfare, and not the beloved's, which is being sought when lovers are made into gods. The beloved is not then truly loved. He or she is only the object or tool used for establishing one's own personal worth.

This means that the commandment also has a positive force. To have God alone as the center and source of life and identity allows one to treat other people as the objects of the love of God, channeled as it were through oneself, rather than as objects by which one seeks personal gratification. How then does one respect God's justice and return God's love? It is not done by sitting around attempting to conjure up pleasant thoughts and emotions toward God, but it is done by trusting the identity and value given by God in Jesus Christ so that believers' lives may be spent in loving service of neighbors, parents, children, presidents, and derelicts. To love God, therefore, is to love in a very practical way those people with whom one shares the various circumstances of life. That is what it means to obey God's commandment and to do God's will.

II. *You shall not take the name of the Lord your God in vain.* To take a name in vain is to use it for foolishness or to treat it lightly, as though the one whose name is being used is of no account. For example, to swear thoughtlessly by God concerning all sorts of trivial things or to damn persons or things in God's name is to assume that the invocation of God's name is meaningless because in the end so is God. It is to assume that God is one who has nothing better to do than to follow someone about, enforcing oaths and making good on all of one's trivial curses. That is to treat God lightly.

But there are worse ways of doing that. A name is a reputation, a handle on one's identity. And as noted above, the reputation of the one whose name is *God* is that in Christ God is shown to be both just and merciful. God is reputed to be one whose ultimate response to human evil is blessing (see Gen. 12:1–3 in relation to Gen. 1–11), not merely curse and punishment. Therefore, the most serious form of taking God's name lightly is to represent God as one heavy with justice but not with mercy. For example, when one who is baptized and therefore a member of God's own family, and who by virtue of that family membership represents God and God's reputation in the world, insists on dealing with his or her neighbor with justice but not in mercy, then God's name is treated lightly. When God's son or daughter, and therefore namesake, acts as if he or she were interested only in what is fair and just, God's reputation suffers because God is made to look like that, too.

To seek justice is clearly necessary and required. Justice is, after all, part of God's reputation. But to seek justice without mercy is to testify that God is pitiless and that the death of Christ, in which God's reputation is most clearly evident and operative, was to no effect. Thus, the keeping of the second commandment requires precisely what the first requires; namely, that people love their neighbors, including family and enemies, with the very love of God.

III. *Remember the Sabbath day, to keep it holy.* This commandment has often been understood too narrowly and therefore misunderstood merely as a demand that once a week a person put in an appearance at a worship service or at least tune in a religious broadcast on radio or television. While there is a relationship between attendance at worship and what this commandment requires, this common misunderstanding trivializes God and treats God's creation as if it were a place of no joy.

The Sabbath is a day of rest, a day to be treated as holy and unique. Holiness is ascribed almost exclusively to God in the Old Testament. It is the word which refers to God's uniqueness. In what, precisely, is God unique? God is unique in a capacity for both justice and mercy (see, e.g., Hos. 11:8–9). Justice and mercy are also the key to the meaning of holy time, i.e., the Sabbath. God is described in Genesis 2:1–3 as setting aside some holy time for rest from work, and that is cited in the Old Testament as the model for the human observance of the Sabbath. God is not, however, setting aside this time merely out of weariness. After all, how much work is it to say "Let there be!" and to have it happen? Only the creation of humanity is said in Genesis 1 to have taken even the briefest deliberation, although perhaps it could be argued that already at this point God saw what lay ahead in the story of human beings and decided that this might be the last moment of divine rest. At any rate, we cannot conclude that rest from physical or mental work is the sole purpose of holy time.

God pauses for the sheer enjoyment of the divine work, namely, the whole pleasing creation. God's people pause for the same kind of holy time. It is a time to remember that life is a gift, the product of unabashed desire and pure mercy. It is not a right or something to be protected and sequestered by means of justice alone. The Sabbath is a day to set aside holy time in observance of the fact that

God owns all of time, and since to a human being time is life, it is a time to remember that God owns our lives. Life is a gift, and in God's eyes the gift is for sharing, not for hoarding. It is for sanctifying or sacrificing. That is, life is for making holy by giving it away for love. Thus, once again, to keep this commandment is to love one's neighbor with the very love of God.

It is easy to forget in the workaday world that life is a gift to be given away for love. The marketplace is most often the scene of justice alone. There we worry over what is fair, economical, appropriate, and just. We compete with one another, asking for and expecting only what is fair. But we set aside holy time so as to hear again the word of God, the good news that there is more to God and therefore more to life than what is merely fair. God's ultimate concern is mercy. God has granted it quite dramatically in sacrificing, in giving away for love, the beloved Son. That message, which we hear and consider in the holy time, begins to invade our secular time, the other six days in the marketplace, and our work takes on a new character and meaning. Our lives become opportunities for service. We work as agents of blessing for the merciful God in Christ, and men and women are loved with the love of the creator who blew the breath of God into the beloved creatures.

The Second Table of Commandments

All of the remaining commandments are also kept by loving and trusting God with a whole heart and by loving one's neighbor as oneself. These commandments differ from the first three primarily in their delineation of specific areas of human life and relationships where this love must become practical.

IV. *Honor your father and your mother.* To *honor* God, in the language of the Old Testament, means to treat God as one who possesses *glory*; that is, as though God were heavy with love as well as justice. Throughout the Old Testament, honor is to be reserved for God alone, but according to this commandment God shares this honor with parents. They, too, are interested in more than discipline or fair play among the siblings, or the distribution of allowance money; they too are incurable lovers. We honor our parents by serving and obeying them not out of some blind sense of duty but because we know them to be full of love for us. They are not always fair, and their love is not perfect; but they are nevertheless God's gifts and as such are to be esteemed as long as they live.

This commandment has traditionally been understood to refer to our relationship not only to our parents but to other authority figures as well. In Romans 13:1-7, Paul asserts that all men and women should be subject to the higher authorities, because these authorities have been set in place by God himself and are God's agents for maintaining order in human society. Obviously, however, governments and other human authorities do not always maintain order, govern justly, or seek what is best for their subjects. Such authorities precipitate genuine dilemmas for people attempting to be obedient to God's will as expressed in the commandments. Should a Christian ever rebel against parents or governments who have become unjust and unloving? Obedience to the fourth commandment requires that men and women diligently seek the establishment of justice and order, so that as much as possible all people might live in safety and go about the work of looking out for one another's welfare. Obedience to this commandment also requires, as do all of the others, genuine trust in God's capacity to work justice and to deal compassionately with human beings, both those in authority and those whom they govern, despite human perversions of justice and lack of mercy. Therefore, obedience to this commandment might mean taking part in various activities whose purpose is indeed the establishment of justice and order, so that men and women might act justly and love one another more fervently.

V. *You shall not kill.* There is nothing mysterious about this commandment's intent. It prohibits taking ultimate justice into one's hands and killing as a means of taking revenge. Jesus extends its meaning to include much more than murder for the sake of vengeance. In his Sermon on the Mount, he equates anger and ridicule with murder (Matt. 5:21-26), and would replace conventional "eye-for-an-eye-and-tooth-for-a-tooth" justice with the commandment to love even one's enemies (Matt. 5:38-42).

Why does God forbid human beings to take their own vengeance? Vengeance belongs to God (Rom. 12:19, quoting Deut. 32:35). Why? Because only God is enough of a lover to administer true justice. Jesus suggests that people learn to turn the other cheek, because regardless of the evil which has been done to someone, to kill or harm the offender is still not justifiable before God, either as justice or as an act of love. Murder is an act of pure self-gratification, and neither justice nor love, as God administers them and shares the capacity for them with humankind, has self-gratification as its goal. Furthermore, to hate offending brothers or sisters, to ridicule them publicly, or finally to take life away from them is to place them or attempt to place them beyond the limits of God's mercy or forgiveness. Vengeance and hatred are attempts to place limits upon the love of God, and in the end they are claims that the effect of the death of God in Christ cannot extend so far as to cover the offender.

Keeping this commandment also requires genuine trust in God. One must depend on God's justice as well as one's own position as the object of God's love, so that one need not seek vengeance but instead trusts in God for protection of life and identity. Those who so trust can, indeed, find in themselves the God-given capacity to love enemies and persecutors. To love enemies does not mean somehow to summon into consciousness the range of pleasant feelings associated with loving those who always return our love. Rather, it is to seek the welfare of our enemies as energetically as we seek our own, and to seek even for them the kind of justice which only God can ultimately administer.

VI. *You shall not commit adultery.* In the world of the Old Testament, the sin of adultery was committed when someone had sexual relations with another's spouse. In a strict sense it did not refer to any other kind of sexual activity, although it has gradually come to be understood in a broad sense as a prohibition of virtually all sexual intercourse outside marriage. Jesus goes beyond even that broad sense and states that for a person merely to look at another's spouse lustfully can be adultery. In that case, even fantasy can be iniquity.

Jesus' comments (Matt. 5:28) suggest that adultery is not merely a crime involving the glands or the genitals. The problem with adultery is much more basic. What both Jesus and the sixth commandment mean by adultery might also be called a form of idolatry in which the object of one's sexual desire becomes the focal point of one's life, and the seduction of that person becomes the adulterer's ultimate concern. The adulterer seeks his or her identity and value from that person or from that relationship. "This will finally put some zest into my life," says the adulterer. "Life will be meaningful again."

There are two fundamental problems with such lust. First, it puts the desired party into the position of one's god. Second, it turns the person into an object which is used not only for physical gratification but for gaining reputation, identity, stature, or value in the eyes of some peer group, or merely in one's own eyes. The welfare of the lover, who in such a relationship is not really beloved at all, is of no concern to the adulterer. This can happen, of course, either inside or outside marriage. A marriage license does not end lust, nor does it keep sexual activity from being adultery.

On the positive side, this commandment requires that men and women genuinely love those with whom they have sexual relations. The creation accounts of Genesis depict sexuality as one of God's bright ideas and therefore as something wholesome and beautiful. The expression used in Genesis 2:24 for the union of the man and the woman is that the two become *one flesh*. That is, they share intimately that part of each of them which is most vulnerable, and they learn true compassion. When one laughs, the other feels the joy. When one cries, the other tastes salt. What keeps sexual intercourse and physical desire from being adultery and lust in such a relationship is the overriding concern in each partner for the welfare of the other. Neither is merely an object in the other's eyes, and neither is forced by the other to play the role of a god. The partners are free to be lover and beloved, the true gifts of the compassionate creator to one another.

VII. *You shall not steal.* Like the other commandments of the second table, this commandment also is firmly grounded in the justice of God. It requires justice in the area of possessions and commerce. It forbids not only the armed robbery of banks and liquor stores but also such varied things as shoddy work, cheating, vandalism, and waste of many sorts. The problem with stealing is that in a sense it is a form of murder. One's possessions are either the products of one's own labor or are purchased with the money one has earned by marketing, as it were, one's labor. Labor takes time which can never be relived. To steal, therefore, is to render useless another person's time. The victim of theft might as well have been dead during the time spent producing or earning what is stolen.

The concern of this commandment is not merely the just distribution and exchange of property and wealth. At issue is really not what is yours and what is mine but what is God's. Like life itself, possessions are gifts and as such are meant to be used similarly to the ultimate gift. That is, possessions are for sharing, for sacrificing, for giving away for love. Those who truly trust the creator do not need to have what is the neighbor's in order to survive. The greed or the anxiousness over tomorrow which leads to theft is displaced by the certainty of one's value (Matt. 6:25–26) in God's sight.

VIII. *You shall not bear false witness against your neighbor.* The great importance of personal reputation is the primary concern of this commandment. The narrowest concern has to do with justice, as the commandment originally intended to prohibit perjury in legal proceedings. Obviously, a lying witness can do irreparable damage to a defendant, and no court system can operate justly so long as witnesses cannot be trusted to speak the truth.

This commandment also has a broader scope of concern, as it has been universally understood to prohibit slander, gossip, and various sorts of treachery. All such malicious communication ruins reputations and, like stealing, is a form of murder. To ruin a reputation is to consign the person who now owns that reputation to the realm of the living dead, cut off from the community which is necessary for real living. It is also to speak as though the slandered one is or ought to be beyond the scope even of God's mercy. The slanderer has taken the place of God and has rendered judgment. The problem is especially grievous among Christians. When a baptized son or daughter of God, a member of God's family, gossips about another Christian, he or she gives the impression that God is no more than a judge. At the same time, he or she ruins a name which just happens to be a name joined in baptism to Christ's own name.

Positively stated, the eighth commandment requires that we protect one another's names as zealously as we protect one another's lives. We do not render judgment upon either, because judgment is ultimately God's work. God is the only perfect, ultimate lover.

IX. *You shall not covet your neighbor's house.* X. *You shall not covet your neighbor's wife, or his manservant, or his maidservant, or his ox, or his ass, or anything that is your neighbor's.* To covet is to let a desire for something which belongs to someone else become so dominant in oneself that one subtly prepares for the day when that object can be spirited away. Even should such an occasion never arise, the covetous one is always prepared and therefore always consumed to a degree by such desire. Coveting, therefore, is a form of lust, and self-seeking lust, as noted above, is a form of idolatry which makes one a poor lover. A covetous person truly loves neither the neighbor nor the desired object which belongs to the neighbor. To the covetous one, even as to the lustful adulterer, the desired wives and servants are merely objects for one's own use, and the object becomes the coveter's desired source of identity and value, that is, his or her god.

This last pair of prohibitions once again calls our attention to the demands which the commandments make not only upon human behavior but also upon human thought and emotions. The very things which one does naturally are prohibited by the commandments—when anger leads to harbored resentment, when sexual fantasy leads to lustful obsession, when simple desire leads to covetous plotting. And who can always control that? The law of God, interpreted as we have here, appears to require what is beyond human control. But that is only the beginning of the bad news.

The commandments taken as a whole are an expression of God's will. As such, they require that we love God with our whole heart and our neighbors as ourselves. Paradoxically, the first table of commandments, which appears to speak only of the relationship between the individual and the creator, is kept principally by loving one's neighbor, while the second table is kept ultimately by acting upon one's trust in the justice and mercy of God. Only those who can truly trust God can truly love their neighbor. Those who cannot trust God view the neighbor as merely a competitor, an object for personal use, even an enemy to be murdered by means of hatred, theft, or slander.

The Commandments and Evaluation

Now, back to the subject of bad news. The truth about human beings is that despite sharing the creator's very life, including the creator's capacity for justice and mercy, none of them automatically trusts God to be either just or merciful. The human race is by nature a breed of self-trusters, who feel compelled to make a life for themselves and to redeem their own time from meaninglessness. The establishment of one's own identity, value, and purpose for living is the primary project of every life. It is a game of self-preservation at any cost. Conventional wisdom dictates that if you do not look out for yourself, no one else will do it for you. If God is brought into the picture at all, it is merely for the sake of justice, and even that is somewhat watered down. Mistrusters seem to cling to the creed that the Lord helps those who help themselves. Therefore, it appears that by nature human beings, those unique objects of the creator's great desire, are chronic mistrusters of the creator and are in outright competition for the role of maker and redeemer of life, time, value, and identity.

Even that, however, is only part of the bad news. Given the situation which has evolved from this competition between creator and creature, even should someone try to live by the commandments of the just and merciful God, one finds oneself in a terrifyingly perplexing bind. For example, one of the most obviously destructive forms of competition is war, and once war is begun even a well-intentioned person is in a fix. To kill the enemy is clearly not the most loving activity—and enemies are to be loved, God says. But then, not to kill the enemy will likely lead to the killing of one's comrades, family, or self. One is responsible for those deaths, too, because they might have been stopped. Thus, once war begins, a person is going to be caught in a choice between killing and being killed.

To be born as flesh and blood into a world where there is war is to be born into a game in which the deck is stacked. All courses of action are condemned. That goes for anyone born flesh and blood, even should his name be Jesus of Nazareth and he happen to be born into a world where the Romans require taxes paid with coins bearing blasphemous graven images (see Exod. 20:4-6), and in which defying the government is prohibited by God, too (see Rom. 13:1-7 and Matt. 22:15-22 and parallels). To be born flesh and blood is to be born into the bind of God's commandments as they confront human nature and its results. Moreover, God does not silence or ease the demands of the law because of these impossible binds (Matt. 5:17-20; Rom. 7:7-8). The law stands as a radical accusation against captives of the double binds, whether they be trusters or mistrusters of God, thus compounding the enmity between creature and creator.

The traditional name for the condition of being born a mistruster into a world full of impossible binds as far as God's law is concerned is *original sin*. It is inherited sin. Everyone has it simply by being born into the world as we know it. If God is indeed the ultimately just one, we are in deep trouble as God's competitors and even enemies.

But we have also presumed all along that God is the ultimately merciful one. Therefore, we must speak more of that mercy, specifically as we have just now glimpsed it in the presence of that Jesus of Nazareth whom we have found caught with us in the law's double bind.

4
THE GOSPEL

God, in Jesus, Suffers Justly, for Mercy's Sake

Christian people proclaim through every conceivable medium, from sermons to bumper stickers, that *Jesus Saves*. What they mean is that somehow the life, death, and resurrection of Jesus of Nazareth are the solution to the human predicament.

Men, women, and children are by nature God's competitors and unable either to will or to do the justice and mercy required of them in their relationships to one another. They deserve to be treated accordingly. Because of their lack of both true justice and true mercy, human beings exist in alienation from one another. They are similarly alienated from the creator whose very own breath they share. And they all die having wasted their lives in trying to cope with the futility of that alienation.

How Jesus Saves

If Jesus saves, he saves from all of that futility and alienation from God and from one another. But how did he do it? How can a single life have accomplished all of that, not only for the folks of his own day but, as Christians confess, for all men, women, and children of every time and place? The technical term for the discussion and examination of that question is *soteriology*, the teaching about salvation.

What one discovers when one begins to dabble in soteriology and probe the question of how Jesus saves is that there are many theories and sets of imagery by which Christians in the past have offered answers and explanations. For example, the New Testament offers several portraits, or images, which represent the earliest descriptions of how Jesus saves. When Paul speaks of Jesus' blood as the price paid for the redemption of sinners (Rom. 3:23-25), his imagery suggests that humanity was in bondage to some alien power. Humanity would be released from bondage only if a payment were made, and that payment is the life of Jesus. Elsewhere, Paul speaks of Jesus as one who reconciles two warring parties, God and humankind, thus bringing peace and new life for humanity (Col. 1:15-23). Several other New Testament authors similarly describe the process as one in which Jesus mediates a new covenant to replace the older covenant which was made at Sinai and has been broken every day since (see especially 1 Tim. 2:3-6; Heb. 8-9). The author of Hebrews describes Jesus as a perfect high priest in the ancient Jewish sacrificial system, who is able by reason of his perfection to offer up sacrifices to God so that God is moved to forgive the sins of those for whom Jesus prays (Heb. 4:14—5:10).

A whole range of additional theories and accompanying sets of imagery was developed during the early centuries of the Christian era, including pictures as bizarre as that in which Jesus is described as a kind of bait, dangled before Satan. When Satan cannot resist any longer and gobbles up Jesus, unaware of precisely what he is eating, he is destroyed by the one he has eaten and Jesus escapes along with all others who have been similarly consumed.

In a way, all of these differing pictures are portraits of the same work of Jesus. They are all attempts to explain what finally cannot be adequately explained with human words. And yet all of them do in fact represent separate theories concerning precisely how Jesus saves. Is it then possible to explain how salvation worked or works without the use of portraits or imagery? Probably not, inasmuch as all human language is, in effect, a system of portraits and images. It is instructive, however, to read the accounts of Jesus' life, death, and resurrection in the New Testament gospels and to attempt to develop our own notion and theory of how it works. Suppose we begin by examining just why it was that Jesus' contemporaries crucified him. The charge against Jesus was blasphemy (see Mark 14:61-64 and parallels). Let us look, then, at the story of Jesus as the story of a convicted blasphemer—whose execution, it turns out, changes everything.

Friend of Sinners

Jesus' life was much like anyone else's life in the territory of Palestine during the era of Roman occupation. He was born in the village of Bethlehem and raised in the Galilean town of Nazareth. He was probably trained to work in the family business—in this case, carpentry—as were most sons and especially the firstborn. Insofar as can be determined, he had no formal education or training beyond that apprenticeship. He did not remain with the family business, however, and near the age of 30 left Nazareth to travel about Galilee, Samaria, and Judea, the three districts of Palestine, eventually ending up crucified on a Roman cross in Jerusalem at Passover time.

During his travels he had occupied himself primarily with teaching, preaching, and healing the sick. These latter acts are sometimes referred to as miracles. Even in the performance of miracles, and especially in his role as an itinerant teacher, Jesus was not unique. There are many accounts of others in the Roman empire of the first century A.D. who healed the sick and even raised the dead, and the world was full of wanderers who fancied themselves as prophets and philosophers. Furthermore, Jesus did not go about proclaiming himself to be a savior or messiah. What was it that made people come to the conclusion, and claim, that Jesus saves?

Strangely, what Jesus did to get that reputation began with words and acts which gave every indication to most of the people of his day that he was a *blasphemer*. *Blasphemy* (in Greek) suggests defamation or injury to the reputation of God, and many things which Jesus said and did seemed blasphemous. For example, he referred to God as *Abba*, which in his native Aramaic language meant *Daddy*. He did this especially in prayer (Mark 14:36) and even taught his followers to do likewise (Matt. 6:9), so that it became one of the characteristics by which his people were known (Rom. 8:15-16).

It is difficult to imagine a pious Jew of Jesus' day hearing such talk without judging it to be blasphemy. So great was the respect for God's name in that culture, a respect grounded in the commandment against taking God's name in vain, that pious Jews did not ever say it aloud. They spoke of God in polite euphemisms such as "Master of the Universe" or "He Whose Name Makes the Hair on the Back of the Neck Stand on End." By rabbinic law, anyone heard uttering the name of God aloud was to be stoned to death for the sin of blasphemy. And yet this Jesus referred to God as Abba— using a family nickname by which children addressed their father. True, he was not stoned for this offensive familiarity, but the authorities could scarcely have approved.

Mark 2:23-28 relates another incident which must surely have reinforced Jesus' reputation as a blasphemer. It seems that Jesus and his disciples were picking grain to eat on the Sabbath—in clear violation of the Sabbath law. When questioned concerning his actions, Jesus replied that, in the first place, he was hungry; in the second place, he had precedent (David had done something similar in Old Testament days), and in the third place, the Sabbath was made for people, not people for the Sabbath. And finally, Jesus says, "the Son of man is lord even of the Sabbath." Those who questioned him concerning this could see him only as another traveling teacher. Were they to consider this person lord of the Sabbath day? Blasphemy!

Also blasphemous in the eyes of his contemporaries was Jesus' practice of forgiving the sins of people whose sins were especially grievous but who had in no way wronged him personally (see, e.g., Matt. 9:1-8). According to the Old Testament, only God can forgive sins against God's law, and a common belief among first-century Jews was that God would withhold forgiveness for truly serious offenses until the end of time. Here this Jesus was claiming the authority to forgive sins. How else could that be interpreted except as blasphemy?

Still another common practice of Jesus raised many an eyebrow in his day. Matthew 9:9-13 is typical of stories in the gospels which tell of the reaction people had to Jesus' frequent meals in the homes of tax collectors and public sinners. Such behavior was considered to be much worse than a minor indiscretion. To enter someone's home, and especially to eat and drink with that person, was to announce publicly that you considered yourself the kind of person your host was. The tax collectors were regarded as Gentiles because they worked directly for the Romans, who held Israel captive and thus kept the promises of God concerning Israel's freedom from being fulfilled. The Romans were therefore considered God's enemies as well as Israel's, and so were their agents, the tax collectors. So, too, were all those who associated or ate with them. To eat with such folk or with public sinners of various sorts was to become *unclean* or *impure*, a term which meant that one was ineligible for the proper and required worship of God. Moreover, such a person was to be ostracized from the community of pious Jews. Jesus was clearly a friend of sinners, and by his actions he publicly counted himself among them as *impure*.

To some extent, it may be said that Jesus committed blasphemy only in the eyes of his contemporaries. For example, Jesus explains (Mark 3:1-6) that his accusers have seen only the justice in the will of God and have missed the mercy. Nevertheless, those accusers could quite justly say of Jesus' blasphemy, "We have a law, and by that law he ought to die, because he has made himself the Son of God" (John 19:7). The condemnation (Matt. 26:63-66 and parallels) and execution of Jesus were therefore just and legal. Despite the fact that he, according to the New Testament's description, trusted in God completely and loved his neighbor as himself, the law and its representatives were bound to accuse and condemn him.

That is, the law and its representatives were in a bind. They had to do what they did for the sake of justice. After all, this friend of sinners had said he was the Son of God and had acted as though he wielded the authority of God, but his accusers could see only another man like themselves. How else could such talk be evaluated except as blasphemy? From our perspective, of course, we can see that the law and its agents were caught in the ultimate double bind and were compelled unwittingly to condemn themselves for convicting and executing one who trusted God and acted mercifully. It is from this same perspective that other God-trusters like Paul would say that only faith and not the law could put one right with God (Rom. 3:19-31). But the law left Jesus' accusers no choice except to execute him. Even Jesus himself acquiesced in their verdict. He did not defend himself at the trial when charged with blasphemy, and the sting of the accusation against him may be sensed in his cry of dereliction: "My God, my God, why hast thou forsaken me?"

There were several possible reactions to what had happened. Some simply assumed that the world had been rid of another blasphemer. Good riddance! Others who had seen and heard Jesus as he preached and taught, and who had been captivated by his portrait of the merciful God, might have thought him proved wrong by the circumstances of his own death. Would a gracious God let such a young person die so unjustly? To these people, Jesus was a tragic figure. Still another perspective existed. It was clearly a minority view at first, but it would come to be called the Christian faith. In that view, Jesus had clearly been in violation of the law, but he was telling the truth about himself and exercising authority which in fact he did have. That is, some of his contemporaries had at least entertained the possibility that he was the Son of God. When they had seen and heard him, they had believed they were observing God in action. From this last perspective, the gospels, the letters of Paul, and all the rest of the New Testament and early Christian proclamation were fashioned.

The picture of Jesus as savior results from looking at the life of Jesus from this last perspective. But how does it work? If Jesus is indeed God or the Son of God (and of course that *if* is the most crucial condition in all of Christian theology), then God has in the person of Jesus acted in a manner which is ultimately both just and merciful. God has submitted to the sentence of death under God's own justice, and God has done so in order to be, and because God is, a friend of sinners. To be both just and loving means that God is not only the one who gives the verdict but also the lover of the person judged—if that person is a human being and thus by nature a competitor of God's and also one of those captives of the double bind of God's just law. Therefore, to be just and loving toward such folk ultimately requires suffering and pain not only for the executed but also for the judge and lover. As Hosea said, to destroy your beloved is to destroy your own heart (Hos. 11:8-9).

In other words, Jesus is the savior because in him God has taken on genuinely human flesh and blood, and God is thus in the position of God's human competitors, caught just as they are in the prongs of the divine law. Jesus is caught between the commandment against graven images and the command to obey and honor authorities (Matt. 22:15-22). He can scarcely work healing or do other acts of mercy, because he is trapped by his own justice in such a world (Mark 3:1-6; Matt. 12:9-14). He cannot even identify himself without being blasphemous. As flesh and blood he is caught, even as is every other flesh and blood creature, in God's just law.

Precisely what is gained by God's joining destinies with humanity? How does that make Jesus *savior*? Does it not merely show the ultimate tragedy of human existence? What makes this life effect *salvation* is that it keeps the sin of humanity, the selfish and competitive nature and the double-bind captivity, from becoming an alienating force or barrier between God and humankind. The separation is overcome because God has taken on the burden of the alienation, and the friendship of God and creatures is restored. Justice has been done, as it had to be, but so has mercy in this ultimate act of compassion, this total placement of one in another's predicament.

To view Jesus from this perspective is to see and know that which is hidden from the world and is only seen ambiguously in the *God of human speculation*. Furthermore, in trusting the God who is known in Jesus Christ, one is personally reconciled to God by means of God's befriending mercy. This is the primary assumption of the Christian faith, and it explains what Christians mean when they say *Jesus Saves*.

The Crucifixion as Saving Event

It is important to note, at this point, that the death of Christ as the friend of sinners is the primary saving event. Christians sometimes speak as though it is really the resurrection of Jesus which effected salvation, as though this last, grand miracle had vindicated Jesus as Son of God and had somehow ratified his work and message. But that is to throw people back upon the *God of human speculation*, because one is already quite aware of the power of the creator. If there is a God, then such a being certainly has the power necessary to bring about a resurrection. Yet it was not the power of God which was in question but the mercy or love of that God. Therefore, the Christian faith focuses upon the cross and the death of Christ as the central event of history.

This is the clear focus of the New Testament. It is true that Paul proclaims (1 Cor. 15:12-18) that if Christ is not raised, the Christians are fools, their faith is vain, and humanity is yet in its sins. It is equally evident, however, in Paul's or any other New Testament writings, that the resurrection was not the crucial event in the saving work of Jesus. In Mark's gospel, for example, it is the way Jesus died, praying Psalm 22 rather than cursing his executioners, that brings the centurion to his conviction, "Truly this man was the Son of God" (Mark 15:33-39). That is Mark's way of indicating that this death reveals the truth about Jesus as well as about Jesus' God. John indicates the same thing by having Jesus proclaim the fulfillment of his work not after his resurrection but in the moment that he dies (John 19:28-30). And Paul, who speaks so decisively concerning the resurrection, summarizes his message again and again

THE GOSPEL 61

as the preaching of "Christ crucified" (see, e.g., 1 Cor. 1:18-25; Phil. 2:5-11).

Even in the gospel accounts of Jesus' post-resurrection appearances, Jesus consistently refers his disciples back to the cross as the center of things. When Thomas doubts what his friends have told him about the resurrected Lord, Jesus appears and presents his wounds to Thomas (John 20:19-31). The wounds are the evidence of the crucifixion. They signify Jesus' work as the Lamb of God, who has taken away the sin of the world by means of his death (John 1:29, 35-36; 19:31-37). Luke tells the story of the disciples on the Emmaus road, leaving Jerusalem after the crucifixion and after the rumors of resurrection had begun (Luke 24:13-35). When Jesus joins them, he does not offer them proof of his resurrection and thereby proof of his lordship. Rather, in view of their disappointment over the potential messiah's failure, Jesus explains from the scriptures the necessity of the messiah's suffering and death. Then he is recognized by these disciples in the breaking of the bread—the meal reminiscent of the last supper, a meal which commemorates not Jesus' resurrection but his betrayal, crucifixion, and death.

It is by dying that Jesus saves. What, then, is the function of the resurrection? What does it mean? The resurrection of Jesus is presented in the New Testament as one of the beneficial effects brought about by his crucifixion. God's having joined humanity under God's own justice, thereby sharing the burden of sin and death, has rendered death incapable of holding humanity captive. Death and the fear of death are no longer able to end forever the chances of friendship in true justice and mercy between God and humanity. Thus, Paul speaks of the resurrected Christ as "the first fruits of those who have fallen asleep" (1 Cor. 15:20-22)—a sign, as it were, of what the crucifixion has accomplished. Elsewhere, Paul describes resurrection as a prize granted not only to Jesus for his humble service unto death but also to all of those who are baptized in his name and have therefore taken his crucifixion as the central event of their lives.

Conclusion

What has been described here is yet another portrait to add to all those which have been offered within the New Testament, and later in the witness of the church, as explanations of how Jesus, the Galilean blasphemer and friend of sinners, saves. Somewhat by reason of necessity, brief descriptions of that from which and for which he saves have also been included. In the end, of course, the entire sketch hangs upon a large *if*. If the blasphemer was telling the truth, Jesus saves. If Jesus was or is somehow God, then God is friend of sinners, and if God is friend of sinners, not even the sinners' death can end the friendship.

5
CHRISTOLOGY

Getting the Story Straight and the Promise Trustable

We had hoped that he was the one. . . ." (Luke 24:21). So the two disciples bemoaned their apparent loss to the stranger on the road from Jerusalem to Emmaus. That was their echo of Jesus' own cry of forsakenness on the cross, and of the great shriek with which he died. For the death of Jesus was a death, and deaths are times of bereavement, of mourning, of a reminder that our human condition is hopeless, at best. If Jesus let out a loud cry as he realized that his Abba was not preventing his dying, then surely all those who had come to find forgiveness and hope and a sense of new life in him faced disillusionment and despair in the wake of his death. Yet the first Christians were soon filled with hope and vigor, and they went about proclaiming a glad message in Jesus' name. What authorizes the transition from dumb despair to excited telling of his story as good news in spite of his dying?

Christians have been tempted to point to the empty grave of Jesus as the great happy ending, the ground for preaching a gospel in the name of Jesus. And of course the resurrection does stand at the juncture of despair and hope. But the message of Jesus' resurrection is not so much proof of the good news as it is the good news in a new light and with a new punch. Easter doesn't work too well as a happy ending to the story. According to Mark's gospel, the event of Easter produces the same reaction as the event of Good Friday: the women are struck dumb with amazement and terror! "And they said nothing to any one, for they were afraid" (Mark 16:8).

No, the normal Christian response to our question is to point to the cross on which Jesus died as the key to the good news. St. Paul, for example, tells the Corinthian Christians that he is determined to know nothing among them except the crucified Christ. Though Jesus crucified is an offense to Jews and foolishness to Gentiles (1 Cor. 1:23), nevertheless Paul and the others came to regard the cross as a mark of honor and a focus for their devotion.

Foolishness, indeed! Imagine a new religious group whose central symbol is a guillotine, or an electric chair! And imagine how appealing would be a message about the great good news that some executed revolutionary offered new hope and life to everyone! Yet the cross is worn by many Christians as a badge of honor. Many Christians also trace the sign of the cross upon themselves when they pray, recalling that their lives are lived under that sign. Furthermore, all Christian church buildings have at least one cross prominently displayed, as a focus for the devotion and prayer of the people.

What makes the cross good is found in our reflecting on who got executed upon it. Theologians attach the label *christology* to the church's reflections about the person of Jesus, the attempt to account for the goodness of their good news by pondering who Jesus is or was. One way to put the basic question is this: What shall we do with the suffering Jesus? What is it about Jesus that makes his crucifixion such good news? What is it about Jesus that makes that remote execution of a messianic pretender have any kind of good effect on the human situation, caught as we are in the double bind where it's "damned-if-you-do-and-damned-if-you-don't" in countless and unavoidable ways?

Therefore, we now aim to deal with this very fundamental question at the center of the Christian faith. And in the process, we will reflect on how Christians can keep on telling the story of Jesus in such a way that the "dear holy cross" remains the heart of the message of comfort for sinners.

If Jesus was who he claimed to be, who was he? Or to put the question in the form in which we need to answer it in our time, if Jesus was who he claimed to be, how shall we say who he is? In putting the question that way, we are first recognizing that if the Christian message is really to be gospel or good news for our present situation, it will not do simply to speak in the past tense. Christology needs to account for the present and not merely the past. And second, we are acknowledging that the business of christology is the church's business of saying something about Jesus, rather than a matter of finding sacred formulations which dropped somehow full-grown from heaven. Christology is made on earth, not in heaven. It is at once our grand and modest business of finding adequate ways to speak about Jesus—adequate, that is, for having his story heard as good news by our contemporaries.

The Classic Question

When in the early centuries of the church's existence the question was raised, *Who is Jesus?*, Christian thinkers quickly discovered that it was all too easy to come up with wrong and unhelpful answers. On the one hand, if one answered by saying that Jesus was really some sort of divine being, then simple logic forced one to add that Jesus therefore only *seemed* to be a human being—a classic example of one of the gods disguised in human form, come to earth to accomplish this or that divine mission, and then free to return to the divine realm whence he came. In fact, there are hints in the New Testament that some Christians did think in that way. Ephesians 4, for example, speaks of a Christ who, having descended from the heights to the lowest parts of the universe, ascended once more on high, leading as booty a host of captives. After the first century a number of variations on this theme surfaced in the church, and these may be loosely grouped under the label *docetic* (from the Greek *dokein*, meaning to seem or to appear). In these views, Jesus only *seemed* to be a man; he was really a god, or a divine being of some sort, or at least a superhuman being. In the world views of the time, this was an almost natural way of thinking; after all, the ancient world was full of gods and super heroes, and it should have worked to think of Jesus in those terms, as well.

Trouble is, if Jesus were some sort of superhuman or divine being, and if he only seemed to be a human being, then it would be hard to come up with anything even remotely resembling gospel by telling the Jesus-story. Under those circumstances, Jesus would mean good news only to people who had some sort of direct encounter with him. For us poor folk who have lived in a different age, Jesus would matter in no other way than, say, the gods Mercury or Zeus or Diana, and the stories about Jesus would take on the quality of the myths about the ancient gods of Greece and Rome—interesting, larger-than-life, but finally not very applicable to the problems and possibilities of subsequent ages.

Worse, if Jesus' connection with God is asserted at the expense of his genuine humanness, then the heart of the Jesus-story is robbed of any sense, or even of its reality. Gods do not die. Not really. They only pretend to die, to suffer, to hurt. Like cartoon characters, they get up and walk away, even after the most devastating of accidents. And if the death of Jesus was only playacting in some sort of ancient cartoon movie, then the good news is not good. There is no comfort for sinners.

On the other hand, if one gets straight the connection of Jesus with our common humanity—that is, if one answers the *Who is Jesus?* question by saying that he was really and fully a man—then one has an equally plausible image of Jesus, and one stands in a tradition as old as Jesus' own time. Like the other view, this one, too, was argued and defended by would-be Christian thinkers, and it, too, has its echo in various passages in the New Testament. Here we might think of the instances where Jesus is portrayed as being angry, as weeping, as being hungry or thirsty or tired, as being in anguish or pain, as bleeding, as growing up through childhood and adolescence, as eating and drinking, and as dying and being embalmed and buried. In the early church there were those who meant to be Christian and who insisted that the full answer to the *Who is Jesus?* question was *a man, period.*

Though there were some important differences among the various people and positions, we might summarize all of them by naming them after a particularly outspoken proponent of this position, a certain Arius. Living in the fourth century A.D., Arius argued that Jesus was indeed the Christ, and that he was indeed a superhuman being, but that he was still a creature of God and thus not really God. Arius thereby shared common ground with all those who downplayed the connection of Jesus with God in order to preserve his genuinely human nature.

The trouble with this view is that it, too, robs the center of Jesus' story of any really good news. If the person who died on the cross on Golgotha was only a human being (even a superhuman being), then his death could only be the death of another culprit, another victim of the bind of life under the law, another poor sucker who got what was coming to him. Oh, he might be an inspiring example of selfless dedication, a devotee of noble and high ideals who inspires other people to similar nobility of motive and intention. But he would still be nothing better than an example, a pattern of how good we all ought to be. If Jesus was only a human being, then the justice and mercy of God have not yet reached their final height, and the heart of God has not yet been broken. Then there is no good news for sinners; the death of Jesus is of even less value than the death of Socrates (who at least died nobly), nor is his life and teaching of any more value than that of a guileless fool like Parsifal. The church therefore finally rejected Arius's teaching on the person of Jesus, just as it had rejected the opposite teaching of the docetists.

Classical christology, then, was developed in a lengthy process which reached its culmination in the middle of the fifth century, after a series of major church councils plowed their way through the dilemmas and the mazes created by a wide range of well-intended Christian thinkers. This christology does not make logical or rational sense—or even mathematical sense, for that matter. It asserts that Jesus was competely and fully human, in the same way and with the same results as every other human being (except that, as one who trusted God fully, he was not a sinner). And it asserts that Jesus was completely and fully God in the same way that God is God. Finally, it asserts that this one hundred percent human being plus one hundred percent God adds up to one whole person or individual, with a single mind and will and soul. In short, it says that Jesus combined two natures, divine and human, in one person.

This classical christology made it possible to tell the story of Jesus in such a way that it could come across as good news to the hearers. Because Jesus was a normal human being, bone of our bone and flesh of our flesh, he could be fully and completely under the bind of the law, and he could suffer and die a real death. Because Jesus was truly God, his death could amount to something as good as what the Christian message says it was; namely, that the working out of God's justice on the beloved creature(s) had finally meant that the sentence had fallen on God and that the beloved creature(s) could live and thrive once more under God's blessing.

The difficulty with such christology is its nonrationality. It just doesn't make sense. It doesn't add up: one human being plus one God does not equal one person. No way. Yet for all its difficulty, and for all its nonrationality, it has become the effective and necessary way of speaking about Jesus so as to keep his death a real and fully human death while at the same time having it amount to something of benefit to sinners. It provides a workable answer to the *Who is Jesus?* question, which meets the double test for doctrine: make maximum use of the crucified Christ, and provide comfort and consolation to troubled sinners.

Nevertheless, precisely because of its nonrational character, this classical christology has always been open to question, to debate, and to distortion. It is as if christology were a rubber band which had to be stretched between two hooks, and the hooks were too far apart for the band to reach! As a result, almost all subsequent attempts to speak about the person of Jesus have tended to stress one or the other pole, either the humanity or the divinity, at the expense of its opposite.

The Reformation Contribution

When his contemporary opponents criticized Martin Luther for a wide range of errors, from heresy to doctrinal innovation to "rending the seamless robe of Christ," they were not entirely wrong. The Reformation unleashed a ferment in theological thinking, not least in the area of christology. And the reaction of the guardians of the old faith was not surprising, for the reformers of the sixteenth century did indeed venture to raise anew some of the old questions from the earliest centuries of the church's life.

Luther, to be sure, did not throw the classical definitions overboard—though some of his contemporaries were perhaps more guilty of that charge than he was. In Luther's view—one that was seminal, if not determinative, for other major reformers—it was not so much that he rejected, or even seriously questioned, the classical christological formulations. Rather, he simply developed a fresh set of images—a set of images which grew out of his fresh understanding of what the gospel meant. By his own later testimony, that fresh understanding came about as a result of his discovery of the meaning of the "righteousness of God" in the letter to the Romans. There and elsewhere, especially in Galatians, Luther found the apostle Paul speaking of God's righteousness in close connection with the guilt, i.e., the *curse* or *sin* of Christ. This notion was the decisive element in Luther's view of christology.

The key element in Luther's fresh approach to christology, and the element which left him most susceptible to the charge of repeating the ancient Arian-like heresy, was his focus on the humanity, the weakness, the death of Jesus. Instead of arguing from the premise of classical christology, Luther began from the ancient view of salvation which saw Christ as the victor over the enemies of God and of his people. In Luther's understanding, however, this was a victory which Christ won by undergoing defeat, a kind of overcoming-by-undergoing. In this view, Christ became Lord (*dominus*, as in the English "dominate") by becoming a servant or slave; Jesus dominates his new people by becoming the servant of that new people and the subject or slave of their satanic oppressor. As we shall see later, especially in connection with the enigmatic statement in the Apostles' Creed that "he descended to the dead," Jesus was seen by Luther as having become his people's Lord by suffering the fate to which their guilt had destined them. "He descended," Luther once said in a sermon. "That's what it means that he has become Lord." Elsewhere, Luther argued that the clue to the person of Jesus was the notion that "God made him to be sin for us," that he became the "curse" for us.

There are, then, two somewhat contrasting, if not contradictory, elements in Luther's view of Jesus. On the one hand, Luther sought to maintain the classical christological view; this he did actively and consistently throughout his career. On the other hand, Luther developed his most effective, most characteristic theology not out of the matrix of that classical view but out of the otherwise heretical matrix which had focused on the weak, suffering Jesus—a view which Luther found presented in an authoritative fashion in the synoptic gospels.

Luther thus seems to present a double image of Jesus, and his views have in some ways set the stage for the christological unsettledness that has characterized theology since the Reformation of the sixteenth century. He put it most succinctly when he wrote, "Apart from this man there is no God." Jesus is the "mirror of the Father's heart," showing and conveying God's love to sinners. Sinners can learn the real truth about God in the crucified Jesus, the Jesus who became sin and the curse for the sake of the sinners for whom he died and whose weakness and sin he bore all the way to his death. This Jesus went all the way to death, beyond the limits of this life, so that when we have to go all the way, we will go nowhere where he has not gone and suffered and so become Lord for us.

A christology which is oriented toward these and similar insights from the reformers will therefore have a double focus. First, it will be sure to preserve the classical christological definitions—not as relics deserving devotion as sacred objects but as a clue to what is necessary if the church is to be able to proclaim a trustable promise; not as a magic formula which needs only to be repeated to produce the right effect but as an aid to getting the story straight and the promise trustable. Second, such a christology will also help us to concentrate on the suffering and death of Jesus as the heart of the good news, and to focus on the weak and suffering human Jesus, who as friend of sinners bore the weight of God's just sentence on sinners. For after all, it is not merely the story of Jesus that matters but the story of Jesus told in such a way that it offers the promise of forgiveness and life *for me*.

The Modern Problem

One is tempted to quote the old adage of the Preacher, "There is nothing new under the sun" (Eccles. 1:9), as one surveys the developments in christology in recent centuries. That is not to say that nothing new has been written; it is rather to say that the new things that have been written and the new notions that have been publicized are really only variations on the old themes. In a secularized age christologies begin to sound more Arian than Arius. Jesus looks more and more like an insightful teacher, a fine moral example, a noble and heroic figure, even a revolutionary of sorts. And the corresponding gospel always concludes with the directive: "Now you go and do likewise!" The opposite view might prevail either among adherents of a kind of religious counter-culture or among devotees of the supernatural or the amazing. A docetic Christ emerges, one so much larger-than-life that he is no longer really a human being. A merely divine Jesus is removed from the binds of history, detached from the realities of the human condition, and devoid of comfort for sinners because he could not really die on the cross—at least he could not die a fully human death.

In our day, it seems, the sophisticated theologians tend more and more to stress the humanity of Jesus, as they capitulate to the secularism of our age, or try to make a christology work on the basis of secularist assumptions. On the other hand, the pious faithful seem hooked on Jesus the miracle-worker, Jesus the amazing one, Jesus the divine one—to the point that they are scandalized by the marks of the humanity of Jesus and positively offended when a pastor preaches in such a way as to take that humanity with utter seriousness. After all, we like our heroes. We need our heroes. And woe to anyone who deprives us of them! From Superman to Wonder Woman to Lassie to space-age machines like R2D2 and C3PO, we draw our heroes larger than life.

The gospels provide the antidote to our attempts to treat Jesus as that kind of hero. He died. He died, according to Mark, with a scream of anguish. He lost. Nailed for blasphemy, the friend of sinners suffered the just sentence of the law. He died in solidarity with all the rest of God's enemies. As a messiah, he had failed. All that is anything but heroic.

The New Testament also provides the antidote to our attempts to treat Jesus merely as another human being and thus as teacher or moral example. "God made him to be sin for us." The Son of God, no less! That is the marvel.

The result is a Jesus worth proclaiming as the ground of good news, of forgiveness and life and hope. For sinners. For us.

Working It Out

Because christology is reflection on the person of Jesus behind the message of the gospel, it is necessarily always formal, always somewhat theoretical, and always a bit abstract. Thus, it always needs to be worked out in the actual business of the church's proclamation—not in the sense that one preaches christology but in the sense that one preaches in a way that works out of an adequate christology. The difference is crucial.

As we said at the beginning of this book, doctrine is *not* a set of religious notions which are to proclaimed as the object of faith. Rather, it is advice to proclaimers of the gospel on how to get it

CHRISTOLOGY 73

straight and so to keep the faith. Christology, likewise, is *not* simply a set of propositions which, if firmly believed, will guarantee entrance at the pearly gates. It is rather that which, behind the scenes or between the lines, serves to keep the gospel good. What we have sought to do in this chapter is to demonstrate the kind of reflection that needs to go on, and to show what happens when we do not get it all straight.

Perhaps we can illustrate this by taking a look at the statements about Jesus in the Apostles' Creed. In the translation used by most English-speaking Christians, it reads:

> I believe in Jesus Christ, his only Son, our Lord.
> He was conceived by the power of the Holy Spirit
>   and born of the virgin Mary.
> He suffered under Pontius Pilate,
>   was crucified, died, and was buried.
> He descended to the dead.
> On the third day he rose again.
> He ascended into heaven,
>   and is seated at the right hand of the Father.
> He will come again to judge the living and the dead.

While it would be beyond the scope of this book to offer a commentary on all the statements in this part of the creed, we do need to point out several significant matters, in order to illustrate how christology (or any other doctrinal statement, for that matter) is not itself the object of faith but serves to keep the gospel trustworthy.

The creed teaches us to say, "I believe in Jesus Christ." Trust is in him, the word and promise of God in the flesh. All other statements of the creed serve to identify the Jesus Christ who is trustworthy. Those other statements are not themselves what is believed; they are rather the story of Jesus in miniature, and they instruct us about what the crucial elements in that story are. The creed thus answers the christological question, *Who is Jesus?*, by saying, "He is the one who. . . ."

The faith is like that. God is the one who linked the divine reputation with a motley crowd of people who named Abraham as their father, and the one who let that people drag the divine name through the mud of their sordid relations with other ancient Near Eastern peoples and their favorite deities. God is the one who stuck by the ancient promises to that people. God is the God who in a voice from heaven identified Jesus of Nazareth as the beloved son. And this Jesus is the one who went the way of the cross, all to be *our Lord.* Understood this way, the so-called articles of faith are not really the things we believe; we believe in Jesus, who. . . . And so we tell his story in such a way that it brings comfort and hope to the sinners he chooses to befriend.

The statements about his conception and birth, similarly, do not serve as objects or even obstacles of faith but simply as identifying statements about Jesus Christ. More particularly, they point to his double origin, to his Godness and his humanness: "conceived by the power of the Holy Spirit" makes the Spirit of God responsible for his being, and "born of the virgin Mary" reminds us that he did not drop from heaven in some primitive spaceship or chariot of the gods but that he entered upon life in exactly the same way as every other mother's child—pushed and squeezed out of the womb to cry and breathe and nurse and live.

It is surely striking that the creed shows no interest in most of his life. It moves directly from his birth to his death: "He suffered under Pontius Pilate." This is not so much to suggest that his whole life was one of pain and suffering as to say that what was most significant about his life was that he suffered the execution of a legal sentence upon him. The key to his life, and thus the key to the story of his life, is that he suffered. All the rest, intriguing as it might have been to know more about it, pales into insignificance.

Imagine the possible interest in his childhood and adolescence: Was he emotionally scarred by the questions surrounding the legitimacy of his birth? Did he have infatuations and involvements with young Nazareth girls? Was he a good carpenter's apprentice? With whom did he study? What formative influences shaped him into the kind of person he became? But there is none of that—not in the gospels and not in the creed. Pass it all by. Sum up this life in one word: suffered.

"He suffered under Pontius Pilate." Again, the intention is to direct us to a particular time and place. Here is not a story of anguish in general. Here is no story that took place *once upon a time*. This one took place "under Pontius Pilate." When Pilate was procurator of Judea and administrator of the affairs and interests of the Roman Empire there, then and there this Jesus suffered. The story is datable, locatable, historical. It is a human story, told of the same stuff of which our stories will be told. There are no fairy godmothers, no kindly woodsmen, no gingerbread houses, no mean stepmothers. Jesus suffered as one of us, in our kind of place and our kind of time, under Pontius Pilate, for us—once and for all.

Perhaps the most problematic and troublesome statement in the creed is the one which confesses that Jesus is the one who "descended to the dead." More than any other creedal statement, this one suffers under a cloud of obscurity and a sort of bad reputation. It has been interpreted in the most widely divergent ways, and it has even been removed from some modern versions of the creed, mainly because people simply cannot figure out what they are confessing when they make this statement. Worse, there seems to be no clear text in the New Testament on which it is based. Some have found a basis in the cryptic statement in 1 Peter 3:19 about Jesus going and preaching to the spirits in prison, and others have found biblical warrant in some of the passages in the Psalms (e.g., 16 and 69) about the righteous sufferer going "down to the pit." Scholars can point to the fact that no formal Christian creed before the middle of the fourth century contained a statement about the descent of Jesus, and that the creed which first contained it was prepared by a group of Arian (i.e., heretical) bishops!

Troublesome indeed is this statement. It certainly is inconceivable in terms of our modern understanding of the world and the universe. Like the ascension of Jesus, it just doesn't make sense. We cannot plot the trajectory through which Jesus moved on his way from here to there—wherever "there" is. We no longer believe, as the ancients did, that there is an "underworld" inhabited by demons, evil spirits, and the shades of the departed. No archaeologist expects to find a tunnel which leads to a place called "Hades." Obviously some sort of translation of the imagery of a descent to Hades will be called for. What shall it be?

One important clue to keep in mind at this point is that as a theological statement, the phrase of the creed needs to be given a theological interpretation, and that is not the same as a cosmological or scientific one. And the second clue is in recalling the double test for the adequacy of theological statements, the test to which we have been returning throughout this study; namely, that adequate theological statements will not waste Christ, or let him have died in vain, nor will they fail to offer hope and comfort to sinners.

Can we venture an interpretation of the descent of Jesus to the dead which meets these criteria? Though certainty is hardly a possibility on this much-controverted point, the following is offered as a possible solution: The confession of Jesus' descent to the realm of the dead aims to say that the friend of sinners who became Lord through his suffering of the sinners' bind under God's law is no stranger to any facet of the human condition. Having been crucified and buried, he fully experienced whatever it is that being dead might mean; that is, he also underwent that part of the human predicament. And he did so for the same purpose for which he underwent any and every other aspect of our situation: that he might become Lord for us.

To confess the resurrection of Jesus is to identify Jesus as the one who has death and dying behind him, once and for all. To say that he has risen means much more than that he has *come back to life.* Rather, it means to say that he is the one who has gone through death and come out on the other side. We are given some hints in this direction by what Luke records in Acts 2 as Peter's sermon at Pentecost: by raising Jesus from the dead, God has made him to be both Lord and Christ. Such claims are not made in the New Testament about other resurrections, such as those of the widow's son at Nain or the daughter of Jairus; those people are said to have come back to life in such a way that they had death and dying yet before them. Death was still the last enemy to be overcome when they would be fully conformed to the cross of Christ. But in Jesus's case, things are different. He is the one who has undergone death in such a way as to have overcome it. And thus his promises are not limited by death, as are the promises of every other human being.

Imagine—a death-proof promise! Seen this way, the resurrection is not so much the happy ending which takes away the sting of disappointment at Jesus' death. Rather, it is the terrible and terrifying surprise that this crucified claimant who could not have been the Son of God was and is indeed God's Son. No wonder the women who found the tomb empty on Easter morning "said nothing to any one, for they were afraid" (Mark 16:8). When the truth is out, that God has taken sin and curse and death into his own self in the crucified Jesus, sinners stand speechless and awestruck! So when we confess that Jesus is the one who "on the third day . . . rose again," we are confessing that the whole story truly is good news. The promise which Christians trust is the one death-proof promise in all the world. That is good news indeed!

The next statement of the creed identifies Jesus as the one who "ascended into heaven, and is seated at the right hand of the Father." Thereby, the creed reminds us that the friend of sinners is indeed at the reins of the universe. Far from being absent from them, he is where God is—in control of his world, and ruling it as a part of his love for the sinners he wills to befriend. Like the statement about the descent to the netherworld, the confession of Jesus' ascension makes no sense if it is taken as a cosmological or astronautical statement. The ascension was not like climbing up a ladder. Rather, it is imagery in the service of a profound theological truth: Jesus, who is the sinners' friend, is not a pretender, a wishful thinker hoping that things will turn out for them in the end. He is, in fact, in charge, and he is bringing about that good and gracious will of God which he spoke and lived.

The final statement moves from the past tense of the earlier statements, through the present tense of the immediately preceding one, to the future: "He will come again to judge the living and the dead." The judgment which sinners fear will indeed come about, and the evaluation which produces the ultimate in anxiety will indeed take place—finally, ultimately, decisively, ineluctably.

But the good news is that the judge is the friend of sinners! Those who trust his death-proof promise for life have already heard the judge's final, end-time verdict pronounced on their lives: "Come, O blessed of my Father, inherit the kingdom prepared for you from the foundation of the world" (Matt. 25:34). He, he the friend of sinners, will come to be our judge. So rejoice!

Conclusion

In this chapter, we have sought to show the importance of the answer to the question, *Who is Jesus?* We have said that the answer to that question is the job of the theological enterprise known as christology. We have suggested that the criteria for adequate doctrinal statements about Christ are the same as for any other theological statements; namely, that they must not allow the death of Christ to have been in vain and that ultimately they must provide good news to sinners. After a brief sketch of the formation of the classical view of the person of Jesus, we picked up a clue from the Reformation period in order to keep the christological statements working for people's hope and comfort. And we have commented briefly on the pattern of the christological statement in the Apostles' Creed in order to keep in mind that the object of faith, that on which faith hangs, is the promise of God in the flesh—the Jesus Christ, friend of sinners, who is our Lord. Now it will be necessary, in the next chapter, to talk about that sort of faith.

6
FAITH

Trusting the Promise and Getting in on the Story

Amid the welter of stories being told all around us, and by us, and to us, the story of Jesus stands out as the sort of story which not only includes a promise, but includes a promise not limited or qualified by the grim reality of death. We have been trying to pay attention to what it takes to keep this particular story straight, so that its promise might really be heard and believed by those to whom Christians keep on telling the story. So now it is time to give some attention to the *hearing* of the story—to how it is that people who live after the time of Jesus get in on the story of the friend of sinners. We will attempt to show that what Christians call "faith" is a particular kind of hearing of this particular kind of story and its particular kind of promise.

What sort of hearing hears the story of the friend of sinners as good news? The Christian answer to that question is, simply, *faith*. Trouble is, the word faith, like so many other important and often-used words, has a multitude of meanings and connotations; just to say the word is not yet to say anything clear and distinct at all. We shall need, therefore, to be careful in this discussion if the faith is to be kept! At the outset, though, we can at least tip our hand: by faith we shall mean, basically and centrally, trust in a promise or in a promising person.

We understand faith this way for two reasons. First, when the story of Jesus is told rightly, it comes out not just as a fascinating tale or a curious reminiscence of the past. Rather, it comes out as a story with a promise, a promise that this friend of sinners is also a friend of the sinner that is you. Second, the only way to respond positively to a promise is to trust it. Suppose a teacher could promise a student an A in a certain course, and she could really mean that as an almost completely unconditional promise: no matter what, you will get an A from me. If the student did not trust the promise, he would be likely to hedge his bet by doing the homework anyway, by attending classes more or less faithfully, and by writing the final examination as well. And thus he would not enjoy the benefit of the promise and its potential for freeing him from his academic anxieties. No, the only way to enjoy the benefit of a promise is to trust it, to bank on its truth, to count on the maker of the promise to deliver as promised. That is why we are saying that *trust* is the sort of hearing of the Jesus-story which is called for if the story is to be heard as the good news it means to be.

Now we will attempt to spell out what faith does and does not mean. To do so, we will address two questions: (1) What is faith? and (2) What does faith accomplish? But we need to issue an advance warning about where it all comes out. Faith, understood this way, takes us right into the midst of a discussion of the nature of the church—which just happens to be the subject of the next chapter.

What is Faith?

The history of Christian theology is littered with the broken pieces of notions about what is decisive for faith. And popular piety in our own time reflects both the great diversity of notions about the nature of faith as well as the broken and less than adequate nature of many of them. While we would not be so bold as to claim an exclusive handle on the truth, we nevertheless want to argue that the conception here sketched has an honest claim both on biblical warrants and on a successful meeting of the twin test for theological adequacy which has repeatedly been referred to in this study.

We must first pay attention to a long tradition of usage of the word *faith* in the church, for this tradition has not only determined much of the language of theology over the centuries but also correctly and helpfully distinguished the uses of this word into two categories. Sometimes faith means, like *creed*, what the church confesses about God and Christ and the church. We speak of *the faith* in an objective sense, referring to what is believed. Now although *the faith* is always stated in terms of assertions and propositions, this does not mean that the assertions and propositions themselves are the object of our believing, that is, the things that are believed. What is believed is the gospel, the message about God's forgiveness and love for sinners on account of the death of Jesus. Or we might say that what is believed is the person who relates the message, or about whom the message is told—i.e., Jesus Christ and those whom he authorizes to speak for him. *The faith* in this sense is what we believe, or better, *whom* we believe, and it is often stated in the form of a creed, such as the Apostles' Creed.

On other occasions we use the word *faith* to refer to the subjective side of things, to the act of believing on the part of the believer. "My faith looks up to thee,/Thou Lamb of Calvary" is how one hymn writer could speak of the faith by which one does one's believing. Here the church speaks of faith in an *instrumental* sense; the word faith now designates not the object of believing but the very act of believing itself. This usage is also reflected in the language of the creeds: "I believe in God . . . , in Jesus Christ . . . , in the Holy Spirit."

Especially in the contemporary situation, it is not at all easy to keep clear and straight what the meaning and connotations of the word faith are when used in this sense. Perhaps we can make this more evident if we survey, briefly, what some of the alternatives might be. What does *faith* or *believe* mean in our ordinary, everyday speech? "I believe it is going to rain," we hear ourselves say. Here *believe* means about the same as "I am reasonably but not fully sure; I don't really know for sure." Believing is then about the same as having a hunch. "Keep the faith, baby" is a recurring exhortation which means about the same as "Hang in there, and things will turn out all right." Or the lover says to her beloved, "Believe me, honey, I love you." And she means more than that she is speaking true words, words that correspond to reality. She means that her profession of love for him is a promise that he is thereby invited to trust; that he should count on her and on her love for him.

The last of the instances just cited best illuminates the specifically Christian use of the words *faith* and *believe*, in the sense of the subjective instrument by which Christians believe or have faith. This point was made centuries ago by the classical theologians, when they distinguished three elements in saving faith: *knowledge, assent,* and *trust.* Their point was to say that if a person is really and effectively to believe the Christian message, he or she must first have knowledge of what is to be believed—must know the facts of the story of Jesus, the history of Israel, the depth of the human predicament, and the like. Furthermore, they argued, a person needs to assent to the truth of the statements about those facts. That is, one must be able to agree that the Bible's or the church's report about these matters is correct, and not full of errors. Then in the third place, a person can finally place his or her confidence and trust in those assertions and in the realities to which they point.

This traditional scheme for understanding the nature of faith has much to commend it—not least, the long tradition of its use by Christian theologians. There is a kind of elementary logic about it. After all, I do have to know something about a thing before I can make a judgment about the truth of this or that assertion about it. I also have to be convinced of the truth of those propositions before I can commit myself in reliance upon them. So far so good.

The problem with the traditional scheme of knowledge, assent, and trust is that it easily misleads us into thinking that the doctrinal statements themselves are the object of our believing, and that assertions about God, whether from the Bible or from the church's tradition, provide the ground of our confidence, trust, and certainty for life. As we have been arguing all along, however, doctrine has an entirely different purpose, and faith has a much better object. If, as we have been saying, the Christian message is the story of Jesus, the friend of sinners, told so that its promise is able to be heard, and if the primary aim of the Christian doctrinal enterprise is to keep that story straight, and if that means telling the story so that its promise is heard as good news, and trustable news at that, then faith is first of all trust in that promise. Faith is essentially, characteristically, typically *trust in the promise*. And when you've said trust, you've said it all—all that is crucial and decisive.

There are several advantages in identifying faith, as we have, first and foremost as trust in the promise-element in the story about Jesus. First, such a view of faith keeps it from lapsing into ideology. Second, it preserves faith from becoming merely an emotional or intellectual phenomenon. Third, it corresponds on the subjective side with the notion of *the faith* which we have seen to be decisive on the objective side. Let us look at each of these advantages, in turn.

When faith is understood principally as promise-trusting, it is given a built-in defense against being thought of as an ideology. By *ideology* we here mean a system of thought or a set of ideas which (to borrow the definition of Marx) does not correspond to reality —however firmly that system of thought might be held. The idea is simply this: sometimes Christians have given the impression that their faith is their commitment to a series of otherwise unbelievable notions, like the sinfulness of innocent human beings, or the miracle stories of the gospels, or the immaculate conception of the Blessed Virgin Mary. Christians, in this view, are those (strange) people who, though they ought to know better, nevertheless believe very firmly a series of things which are unknowable and probably unbelievable—but they believe them anyway. Those things they thus believe make up their ideology, while the rest of the world takes an agnostic view of those gullible folk. On the subjective side, such faith is the obviously irrational commitment or devotion to that ideology. It is something people do to hold otherwise uncertain things as certainties, and to be known as the people who do so. In contrast to this notion, the view here espoused suggests that faith is the result of having heard the promise embedded in the story about Jesus, and of having come to entrust oneself to that promise and the one who warrants it.

On the other hand, sometimes faith is thought of as primarily an emotional or intellectual phenomenon. Faith is then what a person feels very deeply. It is little different from feeling that nuclear power plants must be banned, or feeling that American honor is being squandered by a silly foreign policy out of Washington, or feeling that one needs marijuana or alcohol to have a good time. In this view, faith becomes indistinguishable from anything else about which a person happens to have strong convictions—whether those are basically political, economic, or social in nature. And then it is extremely difficult to see one's commitment called into question without having the sense that one's whole religious life is falling apart, as well.

For example, I know a person who feels very strongly that any sincere prayer will be answered, that medical doctors are destroying our health and only chiropractors can really heal our ailments, that the government is selling us down the river, and that we should launch a preemptive nuclear attack on Russia before they do it to us. What strikes me most when I speak with this person is his inability to distinguish what he understands his Christian faith to be, from the other matters about which he feels so strongly. And as a result, a free-wheeling conversation with this person is a very strange experience; somehow, he manages to sound as if an attack on chiropractors is an attack on his faith in Christ.

This misunderstanding of faith is also reflected in the commonly heard adage, "It doesn't really matter what you believe as long as you're sincere about it." Faith is then the same as sincerity. Faith is being sincere in about the same way that love is never having to say you're sorry. Neither one will wash! Who would question the sincerity of a political candidate's desire to be elected? (Though we might well question the sincerity of his or her statements to the voters!) Sincerely held convictions can be dead wrong, and the sincerity of those who hold those convictions does not excuse their error. Lovers may love one another all too sincerely, but they can still wrong one another, still love selfishly, still hurt one another, still need one another's forgiveness. Jesus criticized the Pharisees of his day because they thought their prayers would be heard "for their much speaking," as the old version had it; nowadays we might well observe that it is commonly held that people will have their religious notions approved by God simply because they have held those notions sincerely.

In the third place, when faith is thought of essentially as trust in the promise conveyed in the telling of the story about the friend of sinners, then Christians are simultaneously being taught to keep straight what faith fastens on *to* and what faith fastens on *with*. When that which faith fastens on *to* is seen to be the promise of forgiveness for the sake of the crucified Jesus, then the only thing one can fasten on *with* is trust in that promise. And then we discover, in addition, that the trust with which we fasten on to the promise is never merely our product; it is, in fact, called into being by the promise. I cannot choose to believe something. I can only trust a promise that is already there without my doing and prior to my doing. If faith were my production, created by my own desire or need to have it, then I would not need a crucified Jesus, and I would not really have the certain comfort and hope which his story provides. Such a view fails to meet the twin tests of adequate doctrinal statements.

What Does Faith Accomplish?

In order to speak about what faith is, it has been necessary to say a lot already about what faith accomplishes. And that should not be surprising, since faith-as-instrument is spoken of precisely because of what it does accomplish. For now, then, it should be sufficient simply to offer a couple of handles for getting hold of this point. One of these handles is quite traditional, and the other is more in line with the kind of imagery we have been using throughout this book. The first is to say that faith justifies, or conveys/receives, the forgiveness of sins. And the second is to say that faith is our way of getting in on the story of the friend of sinners. Yet both statements really amount to about the same thing.

Ever since Paul's letter to the church at Rome, Christians have been saying that we are justified by faith. In the sixteenth century that phrase became a slogan for many of the adherents of the movements for reform in the church. By those words, they meant to say that faith, namely, trust in the gospel's promise, brings it about that the sinner receives God's justice and mercy in such a way that the culprit nevertheless lives. That may sound extravagant, yet that extravagance is grounded in the promise which faith trusts—a promise of life instead of death. For if faith receives what is promised, then it receives a great deal. Faith is the one means for responding positively to a promise, of setting into effect the reality that is promised.

We say about the same thing when we say that faith is our way of getting in on the story about Jesus. When I was a youngster, I read with great delight the stories about Paul Bunyan and his great blue ox. I was entertained by them, and I even learned a good deal about human nature as I followed the fantastic adventures of this larger-than-life hero of the north woods. But that story conveyed no promise, and it called for no faith. I was not invited to expect similar marvels in my own back yard. I was not "in on" the story. It is not just that the stories were fiction; that is not the reason why I could not get "in on" the story. The same could be the case also for a true story.

With the story of Jesus, by contrast, it is indeed possible to get "in on" the story. Believing its promise means becoming a character in the story. Hearing its promise with faith brings that story into continuity with my own life, with my own time and place, with my here and now. When the Jesus story is told rightly, his dying deals with my dying. That is the promise. And when I am invited to trust that promise, "Behold, I live." That was the experience of Saul when he was caught up and involved in the Jesus-story on the road to Damascus and in the house on Straight Street there. That was the experience of countless Christians as they heard the words of promise spoken to them, "Cheer up, your sins are forgiven." The story included them. The story includes me. I am in on the story when I trust the promise that it conveys to me. All this, faith accomplishes.

The People in the Story

There is just one small step yet to take, which simply leads us to the next chapter. The story, its promise, and the trusting of it—none of that is a solo operation. The message is told by people who are the contemporary, living bearers of the story, ones who bring that story into continuity with my world. So when I trust the gospel's promise, I find that I am welcomed into a living organism, a community of those who are already "in on" the story. That community is the church, the collection of message-hearers and message-bearers, the organism created by the story of the friend of sinners himself, accomplishing his befriending of me.

7
THE CHURCH

Spirited People Keeping the Story Alive and Keeping Alive by the Story

An early creed, coming perhaps from the middle of the second century A.D., concludes with the words, "I believe in the Holy Spirit, the holy church." Whoever framed that baptismal creed was obviously keenly aware of the fact that the Spirit and the church cannot really be spoken of in separation from each other. You just cannot have the one without the other. We might restate this reciprocal relationship by saying that the Spirit is that which creates the church, and the church is that which is created by the Spirit. Although a circular argument like this one is never an adequate definition of something, it does suggest what needs to be said at the center of our discussion of the Christian community. When this relationship between the Spirit and the church is kept at the center of our understanding of the church, then Christ's death is not wasted and sinners really do get cheered and comforted by the good news.

Suppose that human being/sinner X hears the story of Jesus told in such a way that she hears it with the trusting faith about which we spoke in the last chapter. Suppose, that is, that X becomes a Christian. What then? Why, then she will discover that she is not alone! As the letter to the Ephesians puts it, someone who was dead in trespasses and sin and is made alive in connection with

Christ (Eph. 2:1) wakes up and discovers that she is not alone, but has by coming to faith also come to be a member of a body, a family, an organism, a community. There is no possibility of an isolated, solo-act kind of Christian existence. To be a Christian is to be a member of the "body of Christ" (Eph. 4:12)—that organism which ensures the continued presence of Jesus in the world, both the bearer of his story and the body charged with continuing his mission of forgiveness and service. That means that there is no other way to be a Christian than as a part of this Christ-body, this community which names him as Lord and is animated by his Spirit.

There are, to be sure, a host of images in the New Testament by means of which the church is described and addressed. We shall focus on just a couple of those images. Our selection is not entirely arbitrary, however, for we shall be concentrating on those biblical images which are most congenial for the understanding of the faith which we have here presented. Accordingly, we do not claim to be saying all that can be said, nor even the last word on the subject. And we do not mean to imply that the following discussion is the only good and true way to speak of the church. Our aim is more modest: here is one responsible way to think about the Spirit and the church, a way which makes evangelical sense.

The Spirit and the Church

First of all, the church is the creature of the Spirit of God, the Holy Spirit. Accordingly, the church is not merely an association of like-minded individuals, a gathering together of the separate adherents of the Christian ideology. That might have been possible, had it been true and adequate to say that the faith is the sum total of those otherwise unbelievable assertions and propositions. In that case, the church would be very much like any voluntary association of people; for example, the Rotary Club or the Union League Club or the Citizens Party. And one might expect to find a list of founding members, a constitution and bylaws, and a set of criteria and qualifications for membership. But there is none of that in the New Testament. The church is what comes into being when the Spirit of Jesus Christ goes to work on people.

The best clues for this image are given in the long discourse of Jesus in the upper room on the night when he was betrayed, as recorded in the gospel according to St. John. In chapters fourteen through sixteen, Jesus speaks repeatedly about the Holy Spirit, the *Counselor* or *Comforter* whom he (or the Father) would send to the disciples. This *Spirit of Truth* will accomplish a number of things for the disciples: lead the disciples into all the truth, glorify Jesus, bring to the disciples' remembrance all that Jesus had told them, convince the world of sin and of righteousness, and take what is of Jesus and make it known to the disciples.

Another incident in John's gospel helps us to put this all together with the church. In chapter twenty, the risen Jesus appears to the disciples and after eating with them breathes on them and says, "Receive the Holy Spirit." He then commissions them to carry out a ministry of forgiveness, which he authorizes with the words, "As the Father has sent me, even so I send you." If we then look back in the gospel to see how and where the Father sent Jesus, we shall see how and where it is that Jesus sends the Spirited group of disciples. He was sent into the world of opposition to God to do the Father's work, to glorify the Father's name, to bear witness to the truth, and finally to be glorified on the cross. All of those images in John deserve lengthy commentary, but this much needs to be said: the Spirit creates a community of forgiven forgivers, and that very Spirit of Jesus Christ continues to enliven the community, enabling it to carry out its mission of going to the same places to which the Father has sent Jesus with the message of forgiveness.

In a very real sense, the creation of the church by Jesus' Spirit is a new creation of humanity by the Spirit of God, which recalls the creation stories at the beginning of the book of Genesis. By breathing his Spirit into his community, Jesus re-creates humanity afresh, in his image, just as at the beginning humanity was created in the image of God. Both creation and re-creation are accomplished by the Spirit, the breath of God, the breath of Jesus. And that means that the church is the community which lives out of the life of Jesus. For Jesus' Spirit works in and among the church—solely to make the new creation into what the old creation had ceased to be: the image and reflection of the God who is after both justice and mercy, and who creates a human being who is supposed to do the same.

Another way of understanding this imagery is to recall both the story of the confounding of human languages at the building of the city and tower of Babel and the story of the first Pentecost, when people from all over the Mediterranean world were able to hear the story of Jesus told in language they could understand. At Babel, as the book of Genesis tells the story, human languages became unintelligible; there was no longer the possibility of a common human story. Nation could now rise up against nation, and each would tell a different story, in a different language. At Pentecost, as Luke tells it in the book of Acts, the Spirit created a new thing—the possibility for all kinds of people to hear the one story of Jesus Christ, and thus the possibility for a reuniting of God's creatures into a single people, a single body. That is the story of the creation by the Spirit of God of a new organism, a new community.

The possibilities are delightful—that is, full of delight—when the Spirit of God re-creates and restores the creation. All that was intended by the creator for the creatures is once more made possible. A new creation means a new delight in the world of God's making, a new delight in the culture and art of humankind's making, a new delight in the beauty of God's world and in the leisure and work of God's people. What God at the beginning pronounced "good" and entrusted to the "creatures" in the garden of God's delight (see chapter 3) is now once more given to the people of God—for their and God's delight. This does not mean that Christians will always be happy, or that they will go through life with a silly smile on their religiously happy faces. It does mean that real joy is possible, the joy that comes from restored and healthy relationships between people, with God, and with God's world. And that new creation is delight-full, indeed.

Much popular thought about the church knows nothing of this vision of the church. Instead, it supposes that the church is simply the result of the common religious quest of people, or that it is the place where religious exercises take place, or that it is the guardian of some vestiges of morality, or the gathering of the people who keep their noses clean and their lives relatively free from scandal and offense. Popular views of the church sometimes focus on the building with the funny windows and a steeple, or on the institution and its governance or administration. Such popular views are reflected when, for example, we speak of "going to church" or "joining the church" or being a "loyal church member." In such views, the church is always something other than the person; it is a place to go, a club to join, a leadership to be followed. In any case, Christ has died in vain, and the message of such a church is anything but good and comforting news.

The creature of the Spirit is a community that has a particular kind of spirit. All communities have a spirit. The spirit of a given community is that which gives life and character to the body and expresses that life and character. In this sense, we speak of team spirit, community spirit, school spirit. The church, then, is that community whose spirit is the Spirit of Jesus Christ. That means that the church is, in essence, characterized by the same characteristics which characterized Jesus himself. It goes where he went. It does what he did. It aims for what he aimed for. It forgives as he forgave. It lives as he lived. It serves as he served. His Spirit is its Spirit. It is his continued presence in the world. Nothing less than that will do.

Forgiven Forgivers

The church is about what Jesus was about. In a word, that was and is forgiveness. The story of Jesus is the story of how, and in whom, the justice and mercy of the God who is an incorrigible lover of the creatures were reconciled; how the just wrath of that God fell back on God's own self, on the beloved Son, so that God could have mercy on the befriended sinners. If the church shares in the work of forgiveness, it therefore shares in that which makes forgiveness possible: the cross. That is, the cross is to be taken up by each successive generation of disciples of Jesus, so that each successive generation of people may find its diseases healed and its iniquities borne (Matt. 8:17).

It hurts to forgive. There is no way around that. Sure, you have to swallow hard to be kindly disposed to one who has offended you. But forgiveness is hard and painful mainly because the forgiver must bear the pain and the hurt of the offense that is to be forgiven. To his church Jesus gives the Spirit. He commissions the Spirited community to carry on and carry out the forgiveness of his sinner-friends, and to do so by being his body in the world—and so to share in his own cross. The church will hurt a lot. It will suffer a lot. It will be forced to sacrifice its treasure and even its very life for the sake of the world to which its Lord has sent it.

Accordingly, the church's posture in the world will be that of a servant, like its Lord. Prestige, pleasure, esteem, pomp, and glory are not the marks of the church. Rather, the mark and treasure of the church is, above all else, the "dear holy cross." For that is what it shares with its Lord.

One, Holy, Catholic, Apostolic

Since very early times, the church has been described by some or all of the four adjectives used in the Nicene Creed: one, holy, catholic, and apostolic. Indeed, almost everything that really needs to be said about the church could be summarized in those four adjectives. We will need to comment on each of them.

To say that the church is *one* is to say that there are not two, or several, or many churches. It is inconceivable that the body of Christ should be plural! The Spirit's creation is a unity, not a plurality. There is one Lord, one faith, one baptism, according to Ephesians 4:1-6. It cannot be otherwise. Is Christ divided? Then neither is—nor may be—his church. The community of promise-trusters is one community, with one Spirit. A community that does not have that Spirit is not the church, however much it may claim allegiance to Christ or may preach and conduct rites and do whatever else we usually think of as church work.

To be alive in Christ is to be in the one church. And that oneness is to be maintained eagerly, zealously. Whatever gives the appearance that Christ and his body are divided is evil, wrong, to be done away with. Modern denominationalism is therefore a serious problem and threat, for it supposes that the church is not one. It elevates being Lutheran or Methodist or Presbyterian above being Christian. That is evil. It contradicts Christ's will for his church. It scandalizes, offends, and affronts those to whom the church would bear the message of Jesus. In fact, the very idea of denomination depends on making something other than Christ the crucial and determining characteristic of what it means to be the church. Because that kind of thinking treats Christ as less than ultimately necessary, it wastes Christ. And that, we have been saying, is to violate one of the two basic tests for theological statements. The church is made one by the Spirit, and it needs to look that way, as well. Denominations must make it a high priority to get themselves into the position where they can be saying about one another, "You are the church; we are the church together."

The church is *holy*. Holy means special, set apart, God's own. It does not mean morally pure or upright or free from sin or free from moral error. To say that the church is holy is to say that the church belongs to God and has a claim to, a share in, God's own holiness —that distinctness which makes God a forgiver, one who succeeds in combining justice and mercy. The church's holiness is God's gift, God's gracious call or choice of a people to whose life God's reputation is linked, so that their reputation might be linked to God's. But that gift is also a mandate, a call to the Christian people to be holy; that is, to live out the uniqueness that is their birthright by living as forgiven forgivers.

The church's *catholic* character is its universality, its extension through time and space. The church that exists today is the church that existed in the first century. The church in Grand Junction is the church in the same way that the church in Rome is the church. Or

Zimbabwe. Or Korea. The catholic church is the common Christian church; the catholic faith is the common Christian faith. To maintain the catholicity of the church is a solemn obligation; narrow, sectarian mentality does not accord with the wholeness of the church and its tradition. Christians need so to order their affairs and their life and work as the church that they do not cut themselves off from, or give the appearance of having cut themselves off from, the whole, catholic, commonly-Christian church. That obligation affects their liturgy and worship, their traditional doctrinal formulations and creedal statements and their style of service to the world to which they are sent.

Finally, the church is *apostolic.* It is the church of the apostles, the church created by Jesus' Spirit at Pentecost and spread by the mission of the apostles and their fellow missionaries. It is the church of the apostles' teaching and fellowship, of the apostles' witness to the story of Jesus as the friend of sinners, of the apostles' preaching and healing and forgiving "in the name of Jesus." The apostolicity of the church consists in its adherence to the original apostolic preaching about Jesus. The New Testament documents are the church's contact with that original testimony, and it is precisely in the church's constant and carefully made appeal to those writings that the church preserves its apostolic character.

Gospel and Sacraments:
Saying and Doing the Promise

The church is that particular gathering of believers in which the gospel is preached and the sacraments are administered. From what we have said so far, it should be clear that the gospel is the Spirit's means for bringing the church into existence. That gospel needs to be both preached and enacted if the Spirit's community is to happen. The gospel, precisely as the story of Jesus with all its promissory content clearly exposed for faithful hearing, needs to be proclaimed if there is to be church. As a story with a promise in it, the gospel cannot be merely enshrined or embalmed in dusty tomes. Its very nature requires that it be said, told, proclaimed, narrated, expounded, explained, explicated. That is why the liturgical high point of the first part of the holy communion is the reading of the holy gospel. That is also why liturgical preaching most regularly focuses on the appointed gospel reading for the given Sunday or feast day. Similarly, the church's life comes from the enactment of the gospel, the acting out or doing of the promise in the sacraments. Baptism ritually enacts the death and resurrection of the sinner with Jesus. Absolution ritually restores the believing sinner to the reconciling community. The holy communion enables the community to partake of the life and death and resurrection of Jesus. These sayings and doings are all sayings and doings of the gospel—the source and center of the church's life.

So crucial are these sayings and doings of the gospel for the church's life that the church has regularly committed such preaching and liturgical presiding to the office of the ministry, to ordained servants of God. There are clergy not in order to create two classes of Christians—normal folk and the really holy people. Rather, there are clergy because the life of the church utterly depends upon getting the gospel preached and enacted in its midst. If the gospel is not served in preaching and sacraments, then the life of the church is snuffed out. Accordingly, when the church designates certain persons as its pastors, it is thereby acting to ensure that it is served with the gospel by which it lives.

Unfortunately, at various times and places in the church's life, ordination to the priesthood has been twisted into a source of power and privilege, and ordinary Christians have consequently been seen and treated as second-class citizens of the kingdom of God. Yet ever and again there have been movements to reform and restore the needed relationship between clergy and laity. For the whole Christian community is a "royal priesthood"; the whole community discharges a priestly function before God as they intercede for all people and as they work to offer themselves for the needs of those people for whom they pray. They are, after all, the ones sent by Jesus as the Father had sent him. The service or ministry of the church's clergy is to help make the service or ministry of the people into something shaped and moved by the gospel. In that way, the clergy may be thought of as servants of the servants of God.

Some Perennial Problems in Church-Talk

Just as it is no small task to keep the Jesus-story straight, and just as it is no small task to answer the *Who is Jesus?* question in such a way that a gospel answer is possible, so it is no small task to keep one's talk about the church straight—straight, that is, according to the measuring stick of adequate doctrinal statements: do not under-use the death of Jesus, and do not fail to offer sinners the good news of their ultimate befriending.

Most of the ancient and modern heresies about Christ have their counterparts and consequences in views of the church. To cite but one example: a docetic view of Christ (the notion that the divine or semi-divine Christ only *seemed* to be a real human being) inevitably leads to a docetic view of the church. Just as docetic Christology down-plays the humanness of Jesus, and indeed is embarrassed by his humanity, so a docetic doctrine of the church is embarrassed by the humanness and earthliness of the church. A docetic doctrine of the church (ecclesiology) would focus on the church's spiritual characteristics, on its perfection, on its infallibility in teaching, and on its grand and glorious share in all the good things that are expected to come. It would be embarrassed and offended by the grubby human side of the church, by the constant and evident failure of church and members alike to live up to the requisite standards, by the church's need to get its hands dirty in service to people whom God aims to befriend by and through the church's self-sacrifice. In short, a docetic church does not need to repent and does not need forgiveness; as such, it wastes the merits of the death of Jesus, and it can offer no comfort to sinners. It can only demand more perfection, and that is really bad news.

In contrast to the ultimately bad news offered by a docetic view of the church, an adequate view of the church would keep it clear that the church, as the creature of the Spirit of Jesus and as the bearer of the story of Jesus into the world, has a necessarily human dimension. After all, who else can tell a story but human beings? Who else is there to continue the presence of Jesus in sacrificial, forgiving service to a world of sinners? And who else can befriend sinners, in Jesus' Spirit, but sinners who have first found themselves befriended?

Against all attempts to ground the truthfulness of the church's witness in its own integrity and its own authority, an adequate doctrine of the church would keep in mind that the church is maintained in truth, upheld in its witness and service, by the very gospel which enlivens and enables it in the first place. The church needs to claim no infallibility in its utterances, decisions, or teachings. The maintenance of the church in the truth of the gospel is the work of the same Spirit who called the church into being in the first place. A Reformation confession of the faith asserts that "one holy church will be and remain forever." That would be so only because the church's oneness, its holiness, and its survival all depend on the same thing—the gospel and sacraments which have given the church its life in the first place.

Conclusion

In the church, everything is oriented toward forgiveness. The Spirit of Jesus calls and gathers together a community of promise-trusters and enables that body to be the bearers of the story of Jesus to the world. The Spirit of Jesus becomes the Spirit of the new community, making that new community more than the sum of its parts: nothing less than the body of Christ, the continuation of his presence as friend of sinners. As human as Jesus was human, the church is sustained in its existence by the gospel that created it. Along with the one whom it confesses as Lord, the church is in the world as servant, ready by the sacrifice of itself to embody God's justice and mercy and so to share in the fate of Jesus on the cross. As the family of brothers and sisters of Jesus, gathered and united by the Spirit, the church acknowledges God as *Abba*, its dear Father.

The church lives as Abba's family to be the instrument of God's will in the world. Such a church prays. It preaches and proclaims. It celebrates the sacraments. And so it serves its Lord and the sinners he aims to befriend.

8
CHRISTIAN PRAYER

Words for the Struggle to Live by the Spirit

In several of his letters to the earliest Christians, Paul speaks of a Christian's life as one that is caught up in a struggle between forces which he labels "the flesh and the Spirit." In Paul's terminology, the *flesh* is the natural human inclination to live strictly by the principles of self-preservation. He assumes that human beings by nature seek their own individual pleasure, value, identity, and purpose for living, regardless of the cost or the consequences of that personal quest upon the lives of others. To live *by the Spirit*, on the other hand, is to trust that one's value, identity, and purpose have already been established on the cross of Jesus Christ and have been received personally in the sacrament of baptism. As a consequence, the baptized people need no longer live for self-preservation but may live for the sake of one another. Sacrifice is the mark of the life lived by the Spirit. That sacrifice is not made, however, without a struggle between the Spirit and the old self-preservation drive. Paul describes the battle as it is waged in himself: "I can will what is right but I cannot do it. For I do not do the good I want, but the evil I do not want is what I do" (Rom. 7:18–19).

The Abba Prayer

The fierceness and duration of that struggle have tempted Christian people, not only in Paul's time but still today, to fear that they are losing their grasp upon the faith and upon the baptismal identity to which it clings. That is, people are tempted to doubt the truth of their place in the family as God's sons and daughters because they are unable to live *by the Spirit*. In the resulting uncertainty over identity, the flesh with its drive for self-identification takes the opportunity to compound the evidence which has unsettled the individual believer in the first place. To people in such a condition, Paul explains that one is not left without resources or weapons for the struggle. The Holy Spirit gives believers the power to hang onto their baptismal identity and convinces them of the truth of their place as sons and daughters of God. How? Twice Paul explains that the Spirit does this by having Christians cry out "Abba! Father!" (Rom. 8:15; Gal. 4:6), thus witnessing to the baptismal identity of the one who so cries out. As was discussed earlier in chapter 4, *Abba* is, of course, that family nickname by which Jesus blasphemously addressed God. Paul's point is that the true mark of one's identity as son or daughter of God is the capacity and audacity to address God similarly.

What does it mean to go about crying "Abba"? It is not a mantra by which the consciousness is altered and the signals of the flesh are tuned out. Paul is referring to prayer as the weapon or resource which the Spirit gives, and by which one can both cling to the promise of baptismal identity and live a life *by the Spirit*, i.e., a life characterized by sacrifice. That "Abba" is a prayer-address is clear from the instance in which it is found on the lips of Jesus himself (Mark 14:36), and that the prayer is one which asks for the strength to sacrifice oneself is evident in both Jesus' Abba-prayer and the references to Abba-praying in Paul's letters. Jesus prayed in the garden of Gethsemane shortly before his arrest and subsequent crucifixion: "Abba, Father, all things are possible to thee; remove this cup from me; yet not what I will, but what thou wilt." Jesus, too, is caught in the flesh-Spirit struggle, as he himself explains immediately after his Abba-prayer (Mark 14:38): "The spirit indeed is willing, but the flesh is weak." Jesus prayed that the Father would accomplish his will and that he would do it through him regardless of what Jesus' own will might be in that moment of struggle. The Father's will, of course, was that the ultimate act of justice and mercy be accomplished in the death of Jesus, thereby effecting the forgiveness of sins and restoring the friendship of God and humankind. The accomplishment of the Father's will required sacrifice, as it always does. Paul indicates as much when he not only associates the Abba-prayer with the flesh-Spirit battle but speaks also of the sacrifice which attends the prayer: "When we cry 'Abba! Father!' it is the Spirit himself bearing witness with our spirit that we are children of God, and if children, then heirs, heirs of God and fellow heirs with Christ, provided we suffer with him in order that we may also be glorified with him" (Rom. 8:15–17). In sum, both Paul in his letters and Mark in his portrait of Jesus in Gethsemane suggest that in the midst of the flesh-Spirit conflict the thing to do is to pray; that is, to cry "Abba! Father!"

If we generalize upon these observations and conclude that the New Testament writers assumed this conflict to be the inevitable context of Christian prayer, then we need to comment further concerning such prayer. First, prayer is an expression of trust in one's baptismal identity, and it is made in the face of sometimes overwhelming evidence that this identity is false or empty. Second, such prayer is made "in the name of Jesus," since it is in him that one's identity as a member of God's family is given and known. That is, every baptized member trusts the promise that he or she stands in the same relationship to God as does Jesus, namely, as beloved child and heir. Moreover, when one stands in that relationship, one is an agent of God's own justice and mercy, one of those sons or daughters like Jesus, by whom God intends to have his will accomplished. The son or daughter will therefore be sacrificed for the neighbor.

Genuine Christian prayer is not an attempt to manipulate God or to gain advantage over a neighbor with God's help. Nor is prayer which presents itself as a bargain, which God may accept if he chooses, genuine Christian prayer. Counterfeit prayers are common among Christians, of course, as the flesh also knows how to pray. But the flesh neither trusts God nor is the least bit interested in the welfare of the neighbor, and it therefore seeks only to strike a bargain with God or to have reality altered to please itself. This is why the Spirit must initiate the kind of prayer which requests the strength to go through with the sacrifice for the sake of another. Furthermore, genuine prayer is not the human attempt to make contact with God, as though God were not listening and God's attention had to be gained so that God might act appropriately. The contact is actually made from the opposite direction. By means of the Spirit, God seeks out those who will act as God's agents, and God teaches them to pray because they will need a firm hold on their identity if the Spirit is to win out over the flesh and if the necessary sacrifice is to be made (Rom. 8:26-27). In general, Christian prayer can be described as words, taught by the Spirit of God, for use in the individual's or the church's struggle to live by the Spirit.

The Model Prayer

The prayer which is known as the "Our Father," sometimes called the "Lord's Prayer," is the model for prayer of this nature. It is addressed to God in the familial fashion. While "Abba" is not the expression used, "Our Father" is an address which implies that the one praying is a family member and thus one who comes with the right to call God by the family nickname. That the early Christian church considered this prayer to be an Abba-prayer, such as those discussed above, is evident in the ancient practice of allowing only the baptized to say it, or sometimes even to be taught it. Only those baptized and thus claimed by the Spirit were caught in the flesh-Spirit battle, and furthermore, only they were prepared for the sacrifice which the saying of the Abba-prayer requested and inevitably entailed.

Another indication of this understanding of the prayer is reflected in the practice, begun in ancient times and still used by some, of introducing the Our Father with the phrase, "And now we make bold to say. . . ." The boldness is required not only because one is now joining Jesus in his blasphemy but also because the price of such an association is always sacrifice. Still another reason that boldness is necessary for those who pray the Our Father is that each petition or segment of the prayer asks for God to do the ultimate saving deed and to bring on the consummation of history *now*. Surely boldness of some sort is appropriate when calling down the end of the world.

Hallowed be your name is the first petition or request which follows the address of Our Father. To be hallowed is to be made holy, and holiness in the biblical sense is uniqueness. God's name, like anyone else's, is God's reputation. (Both God's name and God's holiness have been discussed previously in chapter 3.) What this prayer requests, therefore, is that God's reputation be made special, unique. The obvious implication is that it is not presently holy or that it has been damaged and needs rehabilitation. What special reputation of God's was ruined? It was the reputation of one who is known to be infinitely capable of both justice and mercy. It was a reputation which was first gained as a result of God's friendship with Abraham, Sarah, and their descendants, a friendship which God entered into because it held the promise of being an improvement over responding to human evil with only justice, judgment, curse, and punishment.

The crucial biblical text for understanding how God's reputation was first sullied and then rehabilitated is Ezekiel 36:16–32. There the prophet explains that because God in justice had to punish Israel by allowing the Babylonians to exile them in 586 B.C., Israel had made God look common and ordinary to the world. God thus appeared to the nations as just another vengeful deity, whose promises could not be trusted and whose last word to the chosen people was justice. Ezekiel then announces, however, that God is about to act in order to vindicate God's holy name and unique reputation. How? God will gather together the scattered people once again and cause them to prosper. The point is that *God makes God's own name holy* again by showing mercy to the people of God and by saving them one more time. God's last word was not simple justice then, nor is it ever. To pray "Hallowed be thy name," therefore, is to pray for God to do that saving work yet again and not allow judgment to be the final response to humankind.

There is another feature of this and all of the remaining petitions which must be discussed if the full impact of the Our Father is to be understood. The verbs which are used in the original language of the prayer are forms which request—even strongly urge or command—immediate and complete action. In the case of the first petition, this means that one is asking God to act right now, once and for all, to save the people and thus restore God's reputation as a merciful God and Father. In other words, the prayer asks that God would enact the ultimate, consummating salvation and usher in the promised new age.

The first petition of the Our Father is not only a prayer for a dramatic escape from history as the way out of the flesh-Spirit conflict. Ezekiel 36 provides a clue to something more in the prayer. The prophet there explains that God's work of vindicating God's unique reputation includes not only the political restoration of Israel but the breathing of the divine Spirit into them once more, and the replacement of their hard, stony hearts with flesh hearts. That is, God will re-create them in the same manner as was described in Genesis 2, so that they might be like God, both just and merciful. God's people will then be able to do what the commandments require; namely, to fulfill God's will by bestowing justice and mercy upon all humanity. Furthermore, the people will receive a flesh heart. The difference between a flesh heart and a stone heart, of course, is that the flesh heart is vulnerable. It can be broken. It can be killed. And if one has not only the spirit of compassion which seeks both justice and mercy but also a vulnerable flesh heart, that one's heart is bound to break.

That is the secret of God's own heart, as the prophet Hosea described it (Hos. 11:8–9), and it will now be the same for those among whom God's name has been made holy. Their hearts, like God's own, will be vulnerable and inevitably broken for the sake of those who become the objects of mercy: the lost and sick, the old and abandoned, the criminals, and the isolated rich. Therefore, one prays this prayer with boldness because one asks for a broken heart, for God's own capacity for mercy and compassion. One is asking finally to be crucified for the neighbor, just as was Jesus, the one in whom the heart of God is ultimately revealed and in whom the tension of justice and mercy was played out to its conclusion. Thus, this Abba-prayer requests not only the end of time but also God's own broken heart in the meantime. Such a heart is the mark of a true son or daughter of God and is precisely the tool necessary for life in the flesh-Spirit conflict.

Your kingdom come, your will be done, on earth as in heaven. This petition makes a request for the same results as those sought in the first petition. A kingdom is a political entity in which someone rules and where there is order and justice. There chaos is kept at bay so that people may live in peace. In God's kingdom, however, there is not only justice but mercy, too. That is the point of so many of the parables with which Jesus described the kingdom of God. For example, Jesus compared the kingdom to a king who decided to give a grand party for his son (Matt. 22:1–10). The guests turn out to be not those who deserve to be present but the street-walkers, tax collectors, and other low-lifes. It was not fair. Unfair, too, is the grand welcoming party another father gives to celebrate the return of the prodigal son (Luke 15:11–32). By all that is right and just, the runaway should have been banished from the family, and the older, faithful son should have had the party. But then, in God's kingdom, where God rules, things are not done only on the basis of what is fair. Justice and mercy together are the keys to the rule of God.

And in God's rule, justice is not only tempered, but trumped, by mercy. Therefore, to pray that God's kingdom come is to pray that God would once and for all establish God's unique reign of justice and mercy in the world. It is to ask again for the ultimate act of salvation, for the end of history as we know it and the transformation of reality under God's rule.

The point has been made previously that God's will is that men and women be treated with God's own justice and mercy. The will of God is not a deterministic force by which the world and its history is somehow stage-managed or puppeteered. Nor is it a kind of hidden script of what should happen in history, with the task of humankind being to determine how the script reads so that it can be played out on history's stage. Were that the case, one could never know whether or not one was doing the will of God. For example, one would never know, even after many years together, whether one had married the person who was in the master plan or whether perhaps the script had called for never marrying at all. To live in ignorance of such a script but nevertheless under evaluation by it would be a fearful prospect. Rather, the will of God according to the Scriptures is simply this, that all men and women be saved and brought to the knowledge of God's love for them (1 Tim. 2:4). This petition concerning God's will, therefore, with its once-and-for-all verb, again requests God to bring about the ultimate salvation and transformation of history.

For Christians to pray "Abba, Father, thy will be done" in today's world may well mean what it meant for the Son of God in Gethsemane. It may lead to crucifixion, and in any case it will lead to sacrifice for the sake of those to whom God would extend a just and merciful rule. Although it is only fair and even natural that criminals, unkind family members, drunks, and weaklings should be punished and left to die, in God's kingdom there is infinite mercy which overrules what is *only* fair. To pray that God's kingdom would come "in the meantime," that is, into our history, is to ask that we be put into the places of the unloved, so that through us God's just *and* merciful rule might extend to all the places where human beings live. To pray that God's will be done is to ask that every night be our night in Gethsemane and that we, too, might be strengthened to go the way of the cross.

Give us today our daily bread. In its most obvious sense, this petition is a request for the daily provisions necessary for sustaining our lives. Yet even in that request, survival is not the primary issue. The flesh can and will pray urgently and eloquently for that. Instead, to pray for daily bread is to express one's trust in the giver of all things and to acknowledge dependence upon God. One thereby expresses awareness that everything one has is a gift, rather than something earned. To pray thus for daily bread is a form of thanksgiving.

There is another dimension to this petition. The phrase *daily bread* is an attempt to translate into English a very rare Greek word which means literally *tomorrow's* bread. What might it mean to pray "Give us today tomorrow's bread?" It is not a request for plenty nor even a plea related to the modern phenomenon of the credit card economy, in which we have indeed found a way to have tomorrow's bread today, or at least to live today on tomorrow's paycheck.

If we look back into the Old Testament, we recall that point in the history of God's people when tomorrow's bread was an issue. It was during the wilderness wanderings which followed the exodus from Egypt. When the people became hungry, God provided quail and manna, a bread-like substance which appeared on the ground in the morning. The single provision concerning the collection and eating of manna was that one was to collect only what could be eaten during that day. Any manna collected for the following day would turn to worms (Exod. 16:9–36). Unable to have tomorrow's bread today, Israel came to trust and depend on God's daily providence. There was no hedge against the possibility that tomorrow the menu might be blank and the people might starve.

In Jesus' day, the image of Israel collecting manna each day in the wilderness was an important part of the description of the great eschatological banquet, to be celebrated at the consummation of history (see Isa. 25:6–9 for a typical description of that meal). It was believed that manna, or "the bread of the angels," as it was called then, would be served at the messianic banquet, and that there would be no restrictions on how much could be collected. Tomorrow's bread could be had today. The age of living by hope and faith would have passed, and the era of vindication and living by sight would have arrived. Therefore, for Jesus to teach first-century Jews to pray for tomorrow's bread today was to teach them to pray for the messianic banquet and thus, once again, for the end and consummation of history.

This petition, like those before it, also requests deliverance from the flesh-Spirit struggle. It asks for an end to meals which are *not* eschatological banquets. It begs escape from meals which because of the day's disagreements are eaten in silence, punctuated only by the clinking of utensils, by the news from the nearby TV, which makes certain that the ones eating realize the whole world is lost in the same or a similar kind of uneasy silence, or by the idle comments and cutting remarks which define what kind of silence marks this meal.

When one prays for deliverance from such banquets "in the meantime," one is praying that his or her table be the scene of the eschatological feast. The menu remains the same, but the company changes. Sinners and offenders of every type are welcome, as are the poor and lonely of every variety. There is no silent treatment in progress, because each diner is a gift and a desired guest, even those who show up to eat at that table night after night. What changes the meal is the Spirit, who prompts the waiter, who may also be the chef, honored guest, and dishwasher, to cry "Abba! Father!" in the midst of the flesh-induced silence, loneliness, and selfishness, and thereby to transform that night's leftovers into the bread of the angels. As the author of Proverbs said (Prov. 15:17), "Better is a dinner of herbs where love is than a fatted ox and hatred with it." We may indeed eat tomorrow's bread today when we cry "Abba! Father!"

Forgive us our sins as we forgive those who sin against us. This petition, too, has its once-and-for-all imperative verb, and it is therefore a plea for God's ultimate act of mercy, the forgiveness of our sins by which we become whole. The one who prays this prayer knows, of course, that what is requested is also given and given ultimately. In Christ, God has already forgiven all of humankind by taking a place as flesh and blood among the sinners and removing sin and its consequences as a barrier between God and humanity.

And yet this petition is phrased as though somehow the completion of the work of forgiveness is conditional upon factors other than the death of Christ under the law. It sounds as if one is asking to be forgiven only to the extent that one can or will forgive those who have harmed or offended oneself. In a way that is true, but in a way it is not. If forgiveness were conditional in precisely that way, it would certainly be just and fair. Hard hearts should, in all fairness, be denied mercy. But then few, if any, would ever be fully forgiven of their sins. The just and merciful God is crucified in Christ even for those who are unforgiving. Concerning those agents of justice who nailed him to his cross and who were in no way interested in forgiving him for offending them with his blasphemy, he says, "Father, forgive them; for they know not what they do" (Luke 23:34). God is merciful even to the merciless.

Mercilessness is a dangerous business. To have no mercy upon others, and thus to be unwilling to forgive, is to be interested, once again, only in justice and what is fair. But to want only justice, to desire only what a person rightfully has coming, is to call down justice also upon oneself, as Jesus explained so pointedly in the parable of the unmerciful servant (Matt. 18:23–35). Those who wish to live only by justice really want no forgiveness. In their minds, Christ died to no purpose because he need not have died for them, and it is not in the nature of the just and merciful God to force mercy upon anyone. Love and coercion do not mix.

Therefore, the person who is caught in the flesh-Spirit struggle and whose flesh desires only what is just must cry out "Abba! Father!" and be given again God's own vulnerable heart, so that he or she might learn anew to forgive and to be merciful. To cry out for that heart is to ask for sacrifice, since simple justice is so delicious. That is why we keep scorecards on one another, why we nurture and carefully preserve even the most trivial and ancient of grudges with their bittersweet tastes, and why we treasure information which can be used at the most appropriate time for bringing justice down upon the heads of our enemies. They deserve it, after all. It is only fair. Only fair. But to pray "Abba! Father!" is to ask to be put where Christ is put, namely, in the place of the ones upon whom justice is crashing down and whose hearts are broken irreparably in the ruins of their lives. That is the burden which needs bearing and can be borne only by the sons and daughters of the just and merciful God. The bearing of that burden, the sharing of that broken heart, is the forgiveness of sins, and it is the answer to the prayer, "Forgive us our sins as we forgive those who sin against us." That is, "Father, give us, your sons and daughters, your broken heart, and make us forgivers after your own heart." It is difficult to give up the delicious, poisonous diet of sheer justice, but the menu of the forgivers gives life. It is, after all, the eschatological banquet.

Save us from the time of trial and deliver us from evil. The second of these two petitions clarifies the first, even as the petition regarding the will of God clarifies the request that the kingdom come. In the more common English translation, "Lead us not into temptation," the petition sounds like a request that one be kept from the daily flesh-Spirit battles, or at least that one be given strength to wage a successful campaign against the flesh. But this petition, or pair of petitions, is an important indication that what the remainder of the Our Father has requested is the end of time and the consummation of history. *The time of Trial*, or merely *the Trial*, was the name of the period of time just prior to the consummation of history, as expected by people trained in the thought of Jewish apocalyptic (including Jesus' disciples and most early Christians). Apocalyptic thinking had arisen during the disastrous years which followed Alexander the Great's conquering of Israel (332 B.C.) and the subsequent attempt by the conquerors to obliterate Jewish culture and religion. Apocalyptic literature claimed to reveal God's plans for Israel's vindication and victory.

Remnants of the apocalyptic world view can be seen in the New Testament book of Revelation. According to this type of thinking, Satan would be unleashed for a time immediately prior to the end of history, and he would prey upon believers. It was believed that he would be quite successful and that even most of the faithful would fall away and be lost at that time. That period was called *the Trial*, and Satan was portrayed as the prosecuting attorney at that Trial. He would tell only the obvious truth about the believers. He would produce the evidence that they were sinners and hopeless cases, and that on the evidence of their behavior they could in no way be identified as the sons or daughters of God and in the end deserved no mercy. Moreover, he would convince the faithful themselves of this truth, and they would abandon hope. Their faith would be destroyed, their trust pried free from their Lord. It is therefore not surprising that Jesus taught people who expected the coming of such an age to pray for deliverance from the Trial and from the prosecutor, after first teaching them to pray for the end and consummation of history.

Christians need not, however, think in the mode of Jewish apocalyptic before making sense and great use of this last portion of the Our Father. The Trial and the prosecutor are as much a problem "in the meantime" which we inhabit as they were for the ancient disciples. Our trial is the flesh-Spirit struggle, and the prosecutor sounds suspiciously like the voice of the flesh. The scene of the Trial is wherever it is in the world one has gone with a broken heart, the Father's broken heart, and is bearing and sharing the burden of a neighbor, a spouse, a child, a parent. The prosecutor says what the flesh suspects, that it is all a lie. The pain is only justice and is for no purpose beyond that. It helps no one and has no other meaning. The burden should be laid down.

Seldom, however, does the prosecutor speak so formally. The testimonies are usually the voices of despair over broken relationships, and promises never to get involved in them or never to become vulnerable again. They are the voices which cry out that not even God could straighten out this family, this marriage, this mess, and make it again a corner of the kingdom. They are the voices which say that this one could not be the son or daughter of God, because this one cannot bear anybody's burden nor does anyone else appear interested in bearing this one's. This one is a no one, nobody's son or daughter. This one is unloved, unvalued, worthless. The voices are credible and convincing, and the temptation at the Trial is to act accordingly—to lay down the burden, harden the heart, and become a survivor.

At the Trial, in the presence of the prosecutor, the Spirit cries "Abba! Father!" The prayer was fashioned for just this moment, and the Father to whom the cry is made hears, just as he heard the cry of the first Abba-crier, Jesus, "My God, my God, why hast thou forsaken me?" For the broken-hearted, the Father's heart is broken also, and especially for the despairing. Even that pain is God's own pain. He sends the Spirit, therefore, to cry out "Abba! Father!" in that despair, and one is strengthened, reminded of his or her baptismal identity, saved in the time of Trial, and delivered from the charges of the evil one.

But it must be remembered that the prayer really requests deliverance *in* the Trial, *not just from* it. Christians continue to inhabit the battleground of flesh-Spirit as long as they live, and the prosecutor never ceases to indict. Those who cry "Abba!" form the defense in that courtroom. Through them the just and infinitely merciful God, who never abandons the hope that one day all creatures will be reunited as God's sons and daughters, does the work of tracking down the lost and despairing ones. And what a party there will be when the last of the lost ones returns! It will be the eschatological banquet.

Prayer Taught by the Spirit

In a way, each of the petitions of the Our Father is a request for the same actions or results. The situation in which the prayer is prayed is always the same. It is the flesh-Spirit battle, in all of the many forms and arenas in which it is fought by those who are both baptized and living in the world as flesh, bone, and blood. On the one hand, each petition asks for escape from the battle by way of the ultimate victory which is hoped for in the Father's consummation of history. On the other hand, however, each petition requests essential support for living "in the meantime." And such support has already begun as the Spirit motivates the address which begins the prayer. "Our Father," "Abba! Father!" reclaims the baptismal identity of the praying one as son or daughter of God. The flesh lies, as does the prosecutor, by twisting the truth about the baptized son or daughter, but the Spirit cries out "Abba! Father!" and the son or daughter once again hears and clings to the truth. With such confidence or faith, the children of the Father may live in the Spirit and may sacrifice themselves for the sake of a world full of neighbors in desperate need. The petitions of the Our Father all ask for a share of the Father's broken heart, for the Son's cross, and for the Spirit by which one is able to bear them both for the sake of others.

This prayer of the baptized is therefore also the ultimate prayer of the church, which is the whole body of the baptized. It is the church's prayer for the trust and courage necessary to live up to the name "body of Christ" (see 1 Cor. 12, especially v. 27). The baptized, as the beloved children of the Father, are to the world what Christ is to the world. They are called into being and sent into the world as a community which is to bear, to take away, and to forgive the sins of the world, and to do so by giving up their own lives, if necessary.

The Our Father is the authorization by which what is said of Christ in the Second Article of the Apostles' Creed may now be said of the church. Its members, too, are born of both the Spirit and flesh-and-blood women. The baptized suffer, are crucified, die, and are buried. For the sake of the lost ones, they descend even into the private hells of totally wasted lives. But those who are crucified with Christ in baptism also rise with him. And they become the universal agents through whom God administers justice and mercy, even as Christ himself has ascended to lordship as friend of sinners in every time and space and will ultimately judge the world as both the just and merciful friend.

It has been suggested from time to time in Christian history that prayer, specifically this Abba-prayer, is the most appropriate take-off point for the subject of Christian ethics. Disciplined reflection by Christian people on what is right and wrong, what is moral duty or obligation in various situations, is always done in the very center of the flesh-Spirit battle and in the midst of the double binds in which the law of God seems always to place the people who inhabit the real world. The flesh and the Spirit define morality differently, and it is not always easy to determine which definition, and which urges, a believer is hearing. What sounds perfectly moral may in fact be only fair—the fleshly urge for sheer justice. And what sounds like perfect, self-giving love may in fact stem from the same source, because there is a form of cheap, undisciplined love which contains no justice whatsoever and which is merely the flesh attempting a sham of sacrifice without paying the price. It is easy, for example, to give a few dollars to the poor and salve the conscience, when the real problem is the utter lack of true justice which forces so many to remain in the ranks of the poor. It is difficult, and requires great sacrifice, to work for both justice and mercy in that and many other contexts, and in the end, one seldom knows whether what has been done was right or wrong. Whose urges were being followed?

Given these complexities and the relativity of the various situations in which Christians face moral dilemmas, it will be impossible to speak here in any detail to the subject of Christian ethics. However, we should say that genuine Christian ethics begins with the cry "Abba! Father!" in the midst of the flesh-Spirit struggle, and therefore with the trust that the Father will indeed share his broken heart with the petitioner and work justice and mercy through that son or daughter.

A Final Note

It has been an assumption of this chapter that the people who will pray the Our Father are the ones called into the flesh-Spirit fray by reason of being baptized. We have also assumed that the baptismal identity is the ultimate truth about a baptized one. No matter what, that one is the son or daughter of God and the apple of God's eye. Nothing can alter or lessen that identity, regardless of how difficult the flesh-Spirit battle becomes for those who attempt to be to the world what the crucified Christ is. The evidence for that? Cry "Abba! Father!" What you hear is the evidence. It comes straight from the Spirit. Trust it. It is for sure.

9
BAPTISM

Born of the Spirit of Christ into Abba's Family

Near the end of her irreverent novel *Fear of Flying*, in which she portrays the pitfalls of the frantic search for meaning and identity in today's liberated world, Erica Jong writes prophetically: "Life has no plot. . . . At least it has no plot while you're living. And after you die, the plot is not your concern" (New York: Holt, Rinehart and Winston, 1973, p. 311). That suspicion appears to be universal. Men and women everywhere live from day to day expecting gamely that things will settle down and fall into place eventually, and that life will become sensible and predictable. But it never happens. Life is instead utterly unpredictable, and people always seem unprepared for the next episode. There is no plot.

This experience, and the fears which accompany it, prompt men and women to invent plots for their lives so as to make sense of them. For example, sociologist Robert Weiss, in a book entitled *Marital Separation* (New York: Basic Books, 1977), has described the almost universal tendency of members of families which have fallen apart to develop an account of why the marriage failed and the family crumbled. Each family member's account is different, and on the surface the accounts appear to be mere attempts to justify one's own actions and to place the blame for failure upon other family members or upon extraneous, uncontrollable circumstances. But that is not the ultimate purpose of these accounts, claims Weiss. The real function of each account is to enable the person telling the story to deal somehow with a coherent past rather than with a fragmented, inexplicable set of events. The truth of the matter is that the circumstances leading up to the family's trauma were so chaotic, so complex, and so unintelligible as to be terrifying. How could a life so beautifully dreamed and a future so hopefully plotted have so easily disintegrated in the swirling, capricious chaos of reality? Afraid that life ultimately has no plot, people invent plots and continue to tinker with them as circumstances dictate.

In the language of the preceding chapter, it is the flesh, that consuming drive for self-preservation at any cost, which perceives the lack of plot in life and which suggests some story lines by which the self may be given an important and meaningful role. All of the scripts have happy endings, and the flesh always casts the self into the role of hero. One's life is then devoted to making the script turn out to be true.

The Spirit tells a different story, however, and it is that story which Christians may trust as the plot for their lives in the world of chaos. It is the story of Jesus. It has no happy ending. It hardly has a hero, unless of course you consider an obscure third-world prophet and teacher, who was brutally executed, to amount to one. But the story which the Spirit tells does not end with execution. It proclaims that this particular person's execution has produced resurrection and that death does not therefore mark the end of the story. Death is not the proud and ultimate hero in the Spirit's story as it is in all other stories, no matter how romantically crafted and boldly believed.

It is the Spirit's story of Jesus Christ which by faith becomes the plot of every Christian's life (see chapter 6), and it is the concern of Christian doctrine that the story continue to be told in a straight and trustworthy way to every generation. But Christians do not only speak the story so that it may be believed or trusted; they also act it out in the rituals known as sacraments, and the Spirit has promised that in so doing, their actions are the Spirit's own. In these sacramental actions, it is faith which receives the promise of the acted-out gospel of the sacraments, just as it is faith which is called forth by and receives the promise and benefits of the spoken and written gospel of Christian preaching and the Scriptures.

At least some sacraments are performed by almost all Christian denominations. The number of sacraments, the details of practice, and the precise understanding of the nature of sacramental activity all vary from denomination to denomination, however. The term "sacrament," which means "something made holy," occurs nowhere in the Bible. Obviously, therefore, there is no definition of what sacraments are, or should be, to be found in the canon by which Christians measure their teachings. Some ceremonies appear to be authorized and even commanded in the New Testament, such as baptism (see Matt. 28:19), the Lord's Supper (1 Cor. 11:23-26), confession and absolution (John 20:21-23), the washing of feet (John 13:1-17), or the anointing of the sick (James 5:13-15). Other ceremonies became a part of the tradition of the Christian church without their being discussed in the canon. These included the confirmation of the baptized, the ordination of clergy, and marriage as a rite of the church. By the late medieval period, seven of the rituals mentioned here were considered sacraments of the church.

With the sixteenth-century reform movements, however, unanimity on what should be considered legitimate sacraments ended. Various reformers and protesters eliminated the practice of some sacraments because of abuses both real and imagined. Once this had occurred, a number of different views became popular concerning the definition, nature, and use of sacraments in the church. As a result, there are many different sacramental traditions and definitions today. For example, in the Roman Catholic and Episcopal traditions the seven sacraments of medieval times have been retained and are still termed sacraments. Lutherans and certain Reformed traditions retain all or almost all of the ceremonies but refer to only two (or three, if confession and absolution is included along with baptism and the Lord's supper) as sacraments because of the definition of "sacrament" they use. Other traditions have ceased using sacramental language altogether, although virtually all Christian communions practice baptism.

In the discussion which follows, three rituals will be referred to and examined as sacraments: baptism, confession and absolution, and holy communion or the Lord's supper. Our definition of what constitutes a sacrament may be summarized as follows: A sacrament is a rite or ceremony which is instituted or commanded by Jesus Christ in the New Testament and which has attached to it the promise of forgiveness of sins. The intent here is not to imply that the other four ceremonies commonly practiced in Christian churches are not to be called sacraments, or are not appropriate churchly behavior. We have simply chosen to discuss the three sacraments which are particularly suited to the thesis that the sacraments provide a plot for lives lived in the midst of chaos.

The Meaning of Baptism

Baptism is the first sacrament to which most Christians are exposed. What does it mean to be baptized? The word "baptism" (from the Greek *baptizein*) means "to wash." The name of the sacrament, therefore, suggests the first image or story which is acted out in the ritual of baptism. The baptized one is washed and cleansed of some impurity, and as a result is now distinguished from the uncleansed and has been made acceptable as a member of the washed community.

Ritual washing did not begin with Christianity or even with John the Baptist, the forerunner of Jesus (see Mark 1:4–8 and parallels). For centuries, ritual washing had been an important part of the Judaism out of which Jesus and his disciples came. The book of Leviticus contains the description of an elaborate practice of ritual washings, by which people and things which were unclean, or had become unclean due to contact with what was unclean, were made clean again. The uncleanness in question was not a matter of dirt or even, in most cases, of disease. It was rather a category which indicated that which was unacceptable and, therefore, excluded from the community. Thus, for example, Gentiles, people with certain diseases and conditions, and corpses were considered unclean, as was anyone who had come in contact with them. The worst part of being unclean was the enforced ostracism from the community. To be admitted back into the community, and especially to be admitted back into the worshiping community, one had to complete the ritual washings and become clean again.

Christian baptism, then, may be seen as the acting out of the story of the unclean, ostracized sinner being washed clean and being admitted back into the household, once more to join in such simple acts as eating and drinking and being thankful for life. The comment in 1 John 1:7 that "the blood of Jesus his Son cleanses us from all sin" and the portrait of the saved in Revelation 7:9-14 as those who have washed their robes in the blood of the Lamb are examples of this kind of baptismal imagery in the New Testament. It is important to note, too, that in both cases the washing is done not merely in order to clean up an individual but to create a community. Ephesians 5:26, in fact, refers to the whole community, the church, as having been cleansed "by the washing of water with the word." All of the story lines associated with the action of baptism are essentially community stories, not private plots.

A second baptismal image is that which has given rise to the currently popular description of being "born again." New Testament authors speak of baptism as "regeneration" (see, e.g., Titus 3:5), and Jesus himself offers the most vivid description of baptism as birth. John 3 relates a conversation between Jesus and Nicodemus, in which Jesus tells Nicodemus that he will not understand or have a share in Jesus' life unless he is "born anew." Nicodemus is understandably discouraged at the prospect of attempting at an advanced age to re-enter his mother's womb. Jesus then explains that what he means is being "born of water and the Spirit," referring to baptism, and then goes on to teach Nicodemus that by nature one is born only of the flesh and is thus driven solely by the survival instinct. The life of one born a second time, this time of water and the Spirit, is the life of the Spirit. That is, one's story will be Jesus' story, for he is the one whose Spirit now animates the baptized one.

Again, community is important in the image of rebirth, as one is always born of a mother and into a family. (Even in the kingdom of God, there is no such thing as spontaneous generation!) From this image comes the common practice of speaking of the church as *mother church*, since the church is continually giving birth to sons and daughters of God who were conceived by the Spirit.

Closely related to the birth imagery is the death and resurrection story as the baptismal plot. Paul supplies the most detailed use of that imagery in Romans 6:3-4:

> Do you not know that all of us who have been baptized into Christ Jesus were baptized into his death? We were buried therefore with him by baptism into death, so that as Christ was raised from the dead by the glory of the Father, we too might walk in newness of life.

Thus, to be baptized is to know already how the plot turns out. It is not only to be born anew but to have died and to have been raised again. The worst that can happen has already happened. One can imagine that this imagery is the most cherished among those ancients and moderns who practice baptism by immersion. The initiate is dunked and held under momentarily, acting out a drowning, an execution. Then, when he or she is released or lifted from the water, the first deep, gasping breath is the first breath of a newly resurrected one. Again, the baptized are resurrected not into a vacuum but into a community, the body of Christ, that body animated by his Spirit and charged with doing his work, the forgiveness of sins.

In one sense, then, baptism is the acting out of story lines or scripts which have to do with the life of Jesus, and the theory is that by acting them out, Christian people take on his biography. But what makes such joining of stories possible? What keeps the sacraments from being mere games of pretense and ritualized wishful thinking? The only thing which prevents that is the Spirit's promise that it works. Jesus said to do it, and the Spirit is the one who convinces flesh-and-blood folk to trust Jesus. That is the bottom line. If Jesus is Lord, if he, the friend of sinners, is finally Lord after all, he may be trusted, and therefore the acted-out gospel does indeed provide a story line, a plot, for human life in its chaotic context. Life has a purpose, a goal, a climactic fulfillment in the cross and resurrection of Jesus of Nazareth, friend of sinners.

Baptism Is for Life

In addition, we must note that baptism is not a form of magic or something which, like a vaccination, is to be administered in infancy (or perhaps later in life when the vaccine is discovered) and may then be forgotten or put out of mind because the disease against which one is now immune is no threat and is therefore of no concern. The most appropriate way to speak of one's baptism is not "I was baptized" but "I am baptized," and every day the Spirit by which one has been reborn recalls the baptized one to trust in Christ and to do the work of justice and mercy.

It should also be noted that in most Christian traditions people are baptized only once, while in a few an individual can be baptized as often as that person believes necessary. The reason why most Christians baptize only once is that as they undersand it, baptism does not wear off. The Spirit's promise is sure, and the baptized one is God's son or daughter and the apple of God's eye. Period. The promise is not contingent upon the baptized one's feelings or even his or her continuous ability to keep a firm grip on the promise. There would be no comfort in the promise at all if it were only as trustworthy as the individual believer's capricious emotions and nagging doubts. A common practice of many Christians, however, is to make the sign of the cross upon themselves with regularity, thus reenacting the mark of the cross made upon them in their baptism. That is not magic either but a reminder of one's identity and mission. I am baptized, and I am on my way to the cross for the sake of my neighbor. I live under the sign of my savior —his cross.

Furthermore, in most Christian traditions infants are baptized. In some of the traditions which began after the time of the Reformation, people are baptized only when they can understand what baptism means and when they can choose for themselves to become baptized. There is nothing in the New Testament canon which states directly that infants should or should not be baptized. The practice of infant baptism rests instead on the grounds of the twin criteria by which all doctrine has been judged adequate or inadequate in our discussion to this point.

First, although the child has not committed any offense more grievous than disturbing the family's sleep by crying, he or she still needs the forgiveness of sins which baptism offers. The child is not a natural-born truster of God and like everyone else is born into the world full of double binds and no-win situations between the law's prongs. The forgiveness of God in Jesus Christ is necessary even for such innocents. Second, if human understanding and decision were the ultimate keys to the effectiveness of baptism and the forgiveness which it gives, then baptism is robbed of its comfort as gospel, because one could never know if even as an adult one's understanding were adequate. To add human choice and intellect to the equation of what forgives is to suggest that the work of Christ is either partially insufficient or partially unnecessary, and also to rob the believer of comfort. Thus, while believers can be, and indeed are, surely forgiven or saved without baptism (e.g., the thief on the cross; see Luke 23:42–43), it is certainly also appropriate and salutary to baptize infants.

We must note finally that the baptismal ceremony includes asking the baptized one if he or she takes Jesus' story, usually in the form of the Apostles' Creed, to be his or her own story. Infants cannot answer, of course. Usually some adults, generally called sponsors, answer for the child. The work of the sponsors and the baptizing community is extremely important and extends well beyond answering "I will" at appropriate times during the rite. The sponsors and community pledge that they will take the responsibility of teaching the child, or even the adult baptized ones, for that matter, what it means to be baptized. If the child is not taught, then the sponsors and community will have failed the baptized one and are taking the serious risk that the child will grow up treating that promise lightly or even dismissing it as ineffective. And that is a serious matter. To baptize someone is to take that person into a family and to take him or her upon oneself as a responsibility in an ultimate way. Among the baptized, no one's welfare, spiritual or otherwise, is a matter of indifference. The baptized are a family unit created by the Jesus-story, a body; and no part of either a family or a body suffers by having its faith endangered without the whole being directly affected.

Conclusion

To be baptized, then, is to have a plot for one's life. It is the story of Jesus which one joins in those waters. To be baptized is also to be born into a family and to live with the promise that the family and the Spirit by which birth was given will never desert one of its members. To be baptized is also to be brought to trust—already at the beginning of the story—the promise that not even death can end it.

10
CONFESSION AND ABSOLUTION

Keeping Peace in the Family and Keeping the Family in One Piece

The practice of the sacrament known as "confession and absolution" differs widely, if it is practiced at all, among the various Christian traditions. Its conduct is actually quite simple. It consists of one or more Christians confessing their sins to another Christian or Christians and then hearing the word of forgiveness, spoken directly to those who have confessed. To confess one's sins is to name them aloud, either collectively or individually, and to ask for forgiveness for them, in the confidence that they can and will be forgiven by God and the community of Christians who act in God's name. To be absolved is to be loosed from beneath the burden of what has been confessed. Absolution, then, means forgiveness.

In some traditions this sacrament is referred to as "The Office of the Keys," because Jesus described the authorization to forgive sins as the "keys of the kingdom of heaven" (Matt. 16:19). In other Christian communions, most notably among Roman Catholics and Episcopalians, the sacrament is known by its medieval name "Penance," a name which recalls the practice of assigning to the confessing penitent certain tasks to do or prayers to say, in order to assist in the disciplining of one's life in the future. The danger in such a practice is that people are given the impression that by such acts of penance they are earning their forgiveness, at least in part, and that the death of Christ is therefore either partially unnecessary or partly insufficient in effecting forgiveness. Some denominations and congregations retain the practice of private confession and forgiveness, while others practice it only corporately, often in connection with the celebration of the Lord's supper. In still other traditions, the practice of this sacrament has ceased altogether, usually on the ground of arguments used in the sixteenth-century reforms of medieval abuses of the sacrament, and also as a result of the idea of the "priesthood of all believers" popularized during that time. If all Christians may approach God directly and do not need to have forgiveness mediated through a priest, why go to a priest at all or have a cleric pronounce the forgiveness of sins to a congregation?

The History of the Sacrament

In the early church this sacrament was used for two primary purposes. Most often, it was the means whereby those persons known as the "lapsed ones"—that is, people who had cracked under the tactics of persecutors and who had either cursed Jesus or denied him as their Lord and had divulged the names and locations of other Christians—were brought back into the congregation. In some areas they were never allowed back into the congregation, and texts such as Hebrews 10:26-27 in the New Testament reflect that practice. In other areas, however, if they repented and confessed their denial of Christ and their betrayal of their fellows, they were forgiven. The members of the congregation would bear the burden of those actions together. There was precedent for that practice also, according to the New Testament, since even the chief apostle, Peter, was a lapsed one. Three times, under threat of persecution, he had cursed and sworn in denying that Jesus was his Lord (see Mark 14:66-72 and parallels).

The other major use of confession and absolution, especially in the Middle Ages, was for the benefit of those Christians who had not committed a public offense or endangered the lives of the community members but whose consciences were burdened with one or more sins. Confession and absolution was available for such persons who desired to have the community share in bearing their burden in a very direct way, so that the sinner, now unburdened and not so consumed and preoccupied by the terrors of conscience, might be useful to others in the community and be one of the forgivers in that community as well as one of the forgiven. After all, how can one bear another's burden when one cannot even hold up under one's own?

The Images of Absolution

Jesus himself directly commanded his disciples to forgive and to retain (i.e., not forgive) sins: see, for example, John 20:19-23 and Matthew 16:19. Neither of these accounts, however, includes a description of the method by which that is to be done. Other New Testament passages must provide such a description. The sacrament of confession and absolution, like the other sacraments, is acted-out gospel. The setting for the story line of this sacrament is always within a family situation, for it takes place among the baptized, the members of Abba's family. In one way, the plot is very simple. Christians simply act out one of Jesus' great blasphemies. He forgave sins, and he told his followers that they should do likewise. But the script may easily be dressed up with one of Jesus' own story lines about how forgiveness is administered in families like Abba's.

An excellent example is the story known as the parable of the prodigal son (Luke 15:11-32). One of the sons breaks up the family by collecting his inheritance even before his father is dead, and squanders that for which the father had spent his life working. When the full pain of what has occurred finally dawns on him, he determines that he will go back home, confess his sin, and ask to be received back, perhaps not into the big house but at least into the servants' quarters. So back he goes. What he does not know is that the father has been looking down the lane which led out to the main road every day for all of the days his son has been gone, hoping desperately that this would be the day on which he would return. And today, here comes his son up the path! Out he runs to hug him and kiss him, and the son begins to blurt out his confession. He is a sinner against his father and not worthy of the title son. But he cannot even get the rest of his prepared speech out, the part about renting some of the servants' quarters, because the father interrupts him. The father orders the festive clothing broken out of storage, the fatted calf slaughtered, and the party begun right this minute. "We've never quit setting your place at the table, son. Welcome back!"

This is a picture of the church, Abba's family, at work. The work is the forgiveness of sins. The forgiveness is not magic. It is not some formula learned in the seminary by clergy to be spoken only when the laity performs the first half of the rite. It is work. It is the whole family, even the self-righteous older brothers who have a hard time swallowing all of the mercy which keeps overruling the father's justice, bearing the burden of what has occurred in the lives of the family members. In the story line above, the inheritance is blown and cannot be recovered. No one will ever forget the pain of the months during which the son was gone. Father and son might each be needing therapy, in fact, just to cope with the pain. But the family is restored. One who was dead is alive. And so long as the family bears the weight of what happened together, the burden is bearable. It cannot become something which isolates individuals and fractures the family.

Forgiveness is work. It is putting oneself in the place of the sinner, even as Jesus Christ did, and bearing the burden and the pain of the sin. It is living as the wronged party without vindication. It is learning how to share even the pain which I have inflicted upon others, and standing under my own self-righteous condemnation of other sinners.

This is not to say, however, that the Christian's or the church's life consists only in bearing pain and sharing grief. All the story lines in the New Testament which have to do with lost ones returned or prodigals forgiven conclude with celebration and joy.

That is the truest mark of the forgiven forgivers—their joy. It was the joy set before the one who bore the cross and despised the shame of it (Heb. 12:2), and it is the modern Christian's joy as well. Such joy is not a giddiness, or some perpetual high. It is more like the quiet wholeness and peace which the Old Testament describes with the word *shalom*. *Shalom* is the peace of having everything in its proper place, of having the lost found, of the sinners forgiven and restored to God's family.

The church must always remember to keep all of the places set at the family's table. No sin is too heavy for the family to bear, and no sinner is unwelcome at the table. The father's will is that he eventually have all of his children back. When the church plays out this story line, there is also a mother, of course—*mother church*, who by the Spirit has given birth to the sons and daughters who run off, get lost, and rebel. What is true of the father is also true of the mother, when it comes to the children. As Isaiah says, God would no more forget the children than would a mother forget her sucking child or have no compassion on the child of her womb (Isa. 49:15–16). The children are never forgotten by either parent.

Forgiveness as the Church's Work

The work of this mother, and the extent to which she labors to have her children back, is the subject of another of the great forgiveness texts, the one in Matthew 18. A famous part of this chapter is the description of the procedure of church discipline (18:15–17). There it is stated that if a family member sins against another, the matter should first be taken up privately. If, however, the sinner will not hear the other family member, that one should take along two or three other family members to confirm what he or she has to say. Finally, if they are still not heard by the sinner, the matter should go before the whole church (read "congregation, family"). If the person will not even listen to what the whole congregation has to say, then that person is to be treated as a Gentile and a tax collector. This account is easily twisted into something that it is not, and the popular *Living Bible*, which is not really a translation but a paraphrase, has even institutionalized the twisted interpretation. There the text is made to serve as grounds for excluding sinners and for vindicating those who have been wronged. As we said before (see chapter 8), "the flesh" desires only what is just and fair. It also interprets the New Testament for its own purposes.

Several features of Matthew 18 indicate that it has quite a different thrust, and that it is read properly only by those yet crying "Abba!" in the flesh-Spirit battle. First of all, what is it which the church or any of its members has to say to a sinner? Members of Abba's family have certainly not, even by virtue of their baptisms, become wiser or more adept at escaping the law's double binds. To be sure, they have renounced the devil, the world, and the flesh, but they have escaped nary a one. Therefore, they have only one word to say to sinners. It is the just and merciful Father's gospel of the forgiveness of sins.

If sinners do not hear or listen to that word, it is likely that they do not consider themselves sinners. Then, of course, their sins are retained, and they go unforgiven, at least to all appearances. God has, after all, been known to chase all the way to hell after such a one, but we have noted above that God does not force forgiveness and mercy upon anyone, either. God does not coerce. Nevertheless, because rejecting mercy is dangerous business, the congregation or family keeps trying to get the sinner to hear the message of forgiveness for Christ's sake, even if it requires having a congregational meeting in which every last member of the family takes a try at getting the message across in a trustable fashion. If the family cannot be restored even by such a measure, the erring family member should be treated, according to St. Matthew, like a Gentile or tax collector, that is, an outsider.

And how do you treat Gentiles and tax collectors? Another part of Jesus' scandalous behavior was that he continually ate with them and thereby counted himself among them. He joined them on their side of the law. He bore their burden. He never gave up on anyone, it seems. And back home in the family they are still setting a place for the Gentiles and tax collectors at the table, waiting for the day when they will be back and the family restored, and hoping especially that it will happen before the reunion in the eschatological banquet. In the meantime, family members are out hunting for them and eating with them in their places of isolation, reminding them that their place at the family table is still set.

The justification for this reading of Matthew 18:15-17 is the story which precedes it. In 18:10-14 is Matthew's version of Jesus' parable of the lost sheep. There the Father is compared with a man who is willing to leave his ninety-nine faithful sheep in the mountains while he goes off in search of a single lost one. The reason cannot be that the Father has a thing about having an even hundred sheep, since the fastest way to have only one sheep is to leave ninety-nine in the mountains and go trucking off in search of a lone lost one. The Father is hung up on lost ones, not big, round numbers. Matthew suggests that the family learn to operate like the Father, to live by his Spirit, and to have the same incurable hang-up over every single lost sinner.

True, it is neither fair nor just to operate that way, to save the big parties for the return of the profligates. But that is the only kind of parties there are in the kingdom of God. And what about the family members who run away repeatedly, or keep renewing their Gentile status? Matthew has an answer for that question, too, in his forgiveness chapter. Peter asks (Matt. 18:21) how often a family member ought to be forgiven, thinking by all that is fair that there should be a limit somewhere. But Jesus responds that in the Father's family the capacity for forgiveness expands by geometric proportions and in the end knows no bounds.

Confession and absolution, therefore, describes the inner workings of the Father's family. Along with the Lord's supper, it is what keeps the family together. Perhaps we could say that it is what keeps the family gathered for the supper. As a sacrament, it is the *only* thing which keeps the family together, as we noted previously (chapter 7) in discussing the one, holy, catholic, and apostolic church. For the family is not maintained by the will of its members or by its moral superiority. Its glue is the forgiveness of sins.

Forgiveness is work. Furthermore, everyone in the family is charged with that work. It is not confined to particular people or to particular situations. Even when the minister, on behalf of the whole family, pronounces the forgiveness which every member is really empowered to say, forgiveness remains the work of the whole community. The whole family together pledges, in that absolution, that they will in fact bear the burdens of the terrified and aching ones within the community.

And just as baptism is not magic or something to be forgotten like a vaccination, so forgiveness of sins is the whole life's work of a Christian. To forgive is, in a broad sense, to live by the Spirit, to live compassionately, constantly putting oneself in the position of the sinners encountered in every minute of every day. Sometimes the forgiven ones will not even catch on that some anonymous forgiver has done the Spirit's job on them, even as Jesus died for a lot of folks who never caught on to the great forgiveness which took place. Christ died in the place of, and for the sake of, a world which hardly noticed. So it also happens when the forgiven forgivers of Abba's family take their forgiveness out into the marketplace or the prisons or the red light districts. A few, like the centurion in Mark's gospel (15:39), might catch on to the family connection, but most will not. Yet the family members keep on trying and dying, and their story never ends.

11
HOLY COMMUNION

Taking Part in the Fame and the Fate of Jesus

There is probably no other aspect of Christian doctrine over which there has been so much and such virulent controversy as the holy communion. It seems that every available position has been taken at one or another time in the church's history. And the fractured state of contemporary Christianity is in many ways the institutionalization of those various and opposing interpretations of the meaning of the holy communion. As a result, it is simply impossible to discuss this statement in a neutral way. A common Christian consensus is impossible, and any given discussion is bound to leave untouched someone's or some denomination's pet notion of what is really decisive in this aspect of sacramental teaching.

Nevertheless, we shall articulate a view which, we trust, is not only responsive to the New Testament documents but also aware of the controversies as well. Above all, we shall focus on the gospel that is done in the rite. In the process, we shall try to bring to vivid expression the story which is enacted in the eating and drinking that Christians do in response to the mandate and promise of Jesus. And we shall even risk a few suggestions about what all this might mean for the celebration of the holy communion in our churches.

Traditional Trouble-Spots

From the Middle Ages onward, the church in Europe (of which almost all American Christians are descendants) did its theological thinking and its doctrinal formulating according to the terms, language, and logical possibilities of the philosophy of Aristotle. That massive and impressive system of thought provided the tools and the framework for solving many of the knotty problems the church faced in articulating its doctrine and resolving its conflicts with potentially aberrant views of this or that piece of Christian teaching. When it came to putting into words its teaching about the Lord's supper, the medieval church echoed Aristotle's thought about the notions of substance and accident. According to Aristotle, any given object (or person, for that matter) was thought to consist of a "substance," the real thing itself (such as a book, a collection of writing on leaves of paper bound together), and of any number of "accidents," meaning the marks or characteristics of that particular object, which conceivably distinguish it from other similar objects (such as the number of pages, the thickness of the paper, the style of type or writing, or the color of the cover). Applied to the bread and wine of the sacrament, this meant that it was possible to say that the blessed bread, although it continued to manifest the accidents of bread (it tasted like bread, looked like bread, and got moldy like bread), was nevertheless in its substance the body of Christ. Similar arguments described the contents of the blessed cup.

Called *transubstantiation*, this teaching dominated the theology of the sacrament in the high and later Middle Ages. In spite of repeated controversy, it met with gradual acceptance and even official adoption by church councils. Put most simply, transubstantiation meant that, while the accidents of bread and wine remained, the substance of the bread and wine was changed into the substance of the body and blood of Jesus Christ by the action of the priest who consecrated the elements.

In fact, the notion of transubstantiation had a noble and highly important aim. It was an attempt to account for the reality, the actuality, of the gospel promise contained in Jesus' words "This is my body, my blood." Aristotle had bequeathed a way of thinking and speaking which could allow "body" and "blood" in the sacrament actually and really to be body and blood, while, at the same time, consisting of materials that to all appearances were bread and wine. Thereby, so one thought and hoped, the truth of the words of Jesus was preserved, and the reality of the presence of his body and blood could be assured—or at least accounted for.

The reform movements of the sixteenth century were in part unleashed by what are now almost universally acknowledged to be abuses in the sacramental teaching and practice of the time. Trouble was, however, that there was virtually no agreement among the various reform movements about how to repair the damage. Most of the reformers, nevertheless, gradually came to adopt one or another form of a common view, and this view was really still couched in the logic of the Middle Ages. Abandoning the language of transubstantiation, these reformers focused on the possible meanings of the word "is" in Jesus' words about the bread and cup, and they suggested that in some sense *is* meant *represents* or *symbolizes*. Thus Jesus was understood to say, "This blessed bread [which is obviously still bread] stands for, or represents, my body [which is in heaven, at least since the ascension]." The logical problems were thus tidily solved. Eating the blessed bread was thus taken to be a symbolic representation of a spiritual feasting on the body of Christ.

The problem is that this view has not met with agreement, particularly from the eastern churches, the Roman Catholic church, and the Lutheran churches. For our purposes, however, the more serious difficulty with this notion is that it fails to mesh with the results of recent studies of the New Testament documents, and of the background of earliest Christianity in the Judaism of the first century.

So What Is Going On, Anyway?

We now need to account for some of the key terms in the New

Testament narratives about the Lord's supper, and to do so in connection with the background of first-century Judaism, the milieu in which Jesus and the disciples lived and worshiped.

All the New Testament accounts and interpretations of the supper of the Lord agree on this: that it is in fact a supper, a meal. There is eating and drinking going on, the eating of bread and drinking of wine in connection with some particular interpretative words of Jesus (which are sufficiently different in the various accounts as to defy harmonization), and this eating and drinking is done with Jesus. It is all too easy to lose sight of the simple fact—once the focus shifts to the nature of what is eaten, to the question of who may participate, and to the discussions about who may preside over the whole affair—that the holy communion is first of all a meal. All that is said to interpret and explain this ritual dare not lose sight of the fact that we are here dealing with a meal, with eating and drinking in common and with Jesus.

Meals were a significant, even notorious, part of the ministry of Jesus as the friend of sinners. In fact, his friendliness with sinners culminated in his partying with them—and his righteous contemporaries were particularly scandalized by this: "Why does he eat with tax collectors and sinners?" (Mark 2:16). Those contemporaries could be scandalized by such behavior precisely because of what such eating together meant in Jewish society at the time. To eat at someone's table was to announce yourself to be the same sort of person as those with whom you ate, to link your reputation to the reputation of your host and his other guests. It was to say to all who knew of the meal, "Whatever you know about these people, that's true of me, too."

Thus, when a would-be rabbi like Jesus ate in public with sinners, he was linking his reputation to theirs, linking his fame (or infamy) with theirs. By regular table fellowship with all sorts and conditions of people, Jesus publicly demonstrated that he was, indeed, the friend of sinners. And if his critics missed the point, namely, that God had so acted with Israel by linking up the divine name and fame with Israel's, it was nonetheless not lost on the sinners Jesus befriended by such action.

There is more. To drink a toast together, to share a cup of wine, was a particularly significant gesture. In the Old Testament, covenants were often ratified by raising a cup of wine in order to say to one another, "May your fate be my fate, for we are now linked by treaty." A covenant cup (Jesus spoke of the cup as a "new covenant") was a way of enacting a shared fate. If your enemy attacks you, he attacks me as well. If you have to fight to the death, you may count on me to fight to the death at your side. Thus, by combining the notions of a common meal as a way of announcing a shared fame, and of a common cup as a way of announcing a shared fate, the eating and drinking with Jesus that is the holy communion is a linking of fame and fate between Jesus and his people.

There is still more. All the New Testament accounts of the last supper report that Jesus speaks about his body in connection with the bread from which he breaks a piece for all around the table: "This is my body." Since the word for body (*soma* in Greek) means the whole living person, that is, the very being of a person, the person as living creature, this means no less than to say, "Eat this, and you will have my life in you." That is what the first Christians would have understood Jesus to be saying in his words about the bread with which, and for which, he had blessed God. And when, in some accounts, Jesus adds, "given for you," the meaning is very clear: Jesus is the one who gives his body/life in friendship for sinners, for the very sinners with whom he eats and drinks; and by their eating and drinking with him, they come to have within them the life he gave for them.

We can take still another step. All the accounts, in one way or another, link the drinking of the cup with the blood of Jesus. Luke (22:20) and Paul (1 Cor. 11:25) speak of the cup as a new covenant in the blood of Jesus. Matthew (26:28) and Mark (14:24) refer specifically to the contents of the cup as the blood of Jesus. Now Jews do not eat blood; the book of Leviticus prohibits the eating/drinking of blood, because the blood of a slaughtered animal is its life, and the life-blood is for the atonement of the people (Lev. 17:10–16). The life is in the blood, and when blood is spilled, life is threatened or even ended. The blood of Jesus, then, is the life which he pours out on the cross. Drink this, and you have the life of Jesus inside you; you have the benefit of his dying inside you.

There is another clue in the New Testament accounts. Jesus is said to have "given thanks" or given a blessing in connection with the bread and the cup (1 Cor. 11:24). In first-century Judaism, that can mean only one thing: he blessed or gave thanks to God, and he did so in the fashion then current, which was to bless God by reciting what God had done for the people. A Jewish prayer of thanksgiving recited the saving acts of God, both in creation and in the salvation history of the people. Such prayers are extant, both in their Jewish form and in their early Christian form. In their Christian form, they also include, naturally, the recollection of what God was doing in history through Jesus' death and resurrection.

Because of this historical precedent, the prayer of thanksgiving is still the central and decisive form for the eucharistic liturgy, or the holy communion, of many Christian churches. (The element of thanksgiving is also recalled in one of the names given to this sacrament, the "eucharist," from the Greek *eucharistein—to give thanks*.) When we recall that the act of thanksgiving is the same as that of blessing, we are also helped to realize that the object of the blessing is first of all God, and then, only secondarily, the bread and wine which are thereby set apart for the sacramental feast. No hocus-pocus here; God is being thanked.

Another step should now be taken. Jesus said, "Do this in remembrance of me." Remembrance (from the Greek *anamnesis*) is a key element in the understanding of the eucharist, as it was a key element in the Jewish Passover celebration, from which it comes. When Jesus and his disciples ate the Passover meal together, they did what every pious Jew used to; they remembered what God had done on that night at the Sea of Reeds and in the homes of the Egyptians to deliver Israel from bondage. Now, Jesus says that his disciples should bless God with bread and cup shared in common and that, further, they should do this for the remembrance of Jesus. That is to say, we are bidden to recall, to bring to active remembrance, to call into *our* consciousness, the story of what God was doing in the death and resurrection of Jesus as that which God is doing in our own lives—in the Christian message that is the culmination of the story of God's salvation.

Finally, we must not forget that all of this is reported as having occurred "in the night when he was betrayed." The institution of the Lord's supper stands in closest association with what took place on Golgotha on the Friday the church calls Good. The link between the holy communion and the death of Jesus on the cross is an intimate one. To share in the fame and fate of Jesus is to share in the fame and the fate of the Jesus who was crucified. This meal leads to a cross! The repetition of this meal is a constant reminder of that cross. Those who eat it are being sent to a similar fate. Many Christians, therefore, mark themselves with the sign of the cross as they commune.

When Christians celebrate the holy communion, they are enacting all of that. When the church eats and drinks for the remembrance of Jesus, it repeats so as to re-present (that is, make present again) the fellowship of Jesus with the people with whom he links his fame and fate. And when that happens, there is a happy exchange, for suddenly his fame and fate become theirs, every bit as much as their fame and fate become his. The story of the friend of sinners is reenacted for *this* group of sinners, and so the promise of forgiveness and new life is made present for those who eat the bread and drink the cup with which they have blessed God.

Locating the Promise

In the welter of ideas associated with the ritual meal of the holy communion, it is possible to lose sight of the center of it all. Where, for instance, in contemporary celebrations of the supper, is the promise? We prefer to put it this way: as we act out the story of the friend of sinners in table fellowship with sinners, the promise is that he will again do the business of forgiving, just as he did the first time. Also for *these* sinners. Even now. So realism in sacramental theology is at its best when it is aimed at that promise. Realism in sacramental theology is less than the best when it focuses only on substances or accidents, or corpuscles and molecules, on sacred elements and sacred formulae. What needs to be real, or actual, is the promise of forgiveness from the sinners' friend.

Far more than merely symbolizing or only representing the presence of an otherwise really absent Lord, the sacrament of the altar enacts his actual, forgiving presence. That can be expressed with the help of any of the various types of imagery which we have rehearsed in this chapter. What is decisive is the enacting, the doing of the promise about forgiveness, so that befriended sinners can receive and trust it. Really.

The promise, laden here as elsewhere with its appeal to the particular past when the actions of the story took place, nevertheless points also to the future, a future which is itself laden with promise. Eat and drink this blessed bread and cup, here and now, and the promise is that you are marked for being in on the great banquet of the kingdom of God at the last day. When God wraps up the work of salvation, God aims to throw a cosmic party, a eucharistic feast for the celebration of God's own ultimate glory. God and the Lamb and the church-creating Spirit, together with all the saints in light, are going to be present at the party. They will do eucharist together, the greatest of the great thanksgivings. And all the saints will, with one voice, congratulate the Holy Trinity.

Congratulate means "to say thanks together." And that, come to think of it, is what the future of God's people is all about—saying thanks together to a saving God. After all, Jesus said to the disciples in the upper room, "I shall not drink of the fruit of the vine until the kingdom of God comes" (Luke 22:18). The positive side of that statement is his promise that in the kingdom he will indeed drink the cup that links his fame and fate with that of his fellow eaters and drinkers, and that will be the fame and fate of the glorified one, the one whom the book of Revelation calls "the Lamb" who shares the throne of God (Rev. 22:1, 3). The text for the congratulatory toast is given in the book of Revelation:

"Amen! Blessing and glory and wisdom and thanksgiving and honor and power and might be to our God for ever and ever! Amen" (Rev. 7:12). And to the Lamb—who was slain!

Meanwhile, Back in the Present

Finally, we need to consider some of the implications of these reflections for the celebration of the holy communion in our churches. First of all, precisely because the promise of forgiveness and new life is being enacted in the holy communion, faith is called for if we are to participate properly in that feast. Only faith receives the promise. Only faith receives the benefits of the eucharistic feast. People who eat and drink without faith are really saying, "I don't need a crucified Jesus. I don't need the promised forgiveness." Such a person may be ever so pious and ever so dutiful. Such a person may get a tingly feeling all over from participating in the marvelous ritual—particularly if the celebration is by a congregation that is adept at celebration. But only faith receives the promise. Without faith, the story is denied and belied, and the benefits are wasted.

For that reason, the supper is not for everybody. St. Paul had to tell the Corinthian Christians that unworthy participants eat and drink judgment to themselves, precisely when they eat and drink without "discerning the body." By that he meant that those who eat and drink at the Lord's table need to recognize the body as the gathering of forgiven promise-trusters, who are together acknowledging their need of the mercy of God. Participants need to discern that sinners are forgiven by being united with Christ, and united with his life and his death. These are the body of the baptized, the ones whose stories are told together with the story of God's number one beloved Son, Jesus. And so the partakers become joyous part-takers in the fame and the fate of Jesus. Happy exchange, that sacrament.

This meal sends the members of the body forth to link their reputations and their destinies—to the cross. You will recall how after Jesus and the disciples had eaten and drunk together, they sang a hymn and went out—to betrayal and arrest, trial and execution. Linked by a common meal to a cross-bound Lord, Christians are sent from the holy communion into a world where their task is, with that Lord, to embody the merciful will of a God who aims to forgive by bearing the hurt and the affront in God's own self. They leave their feast, forgiven in order to forgive, blessed in order to be a blessing, fed in order to feed. There is no place to hide but no need to fear. They are marked for a common fate with their Lord, and they trust his promise that their fate, like his, will finally be reversed. They die with the Lord; they shall live with the Lord. It's a promise.

The common meal may well point to the cross of Good Friday, but it is a feast of thanksgiving celebrated on this side of Easter. St. Luke reports that in Emmaus the disciples recognized the Lord in the breaking of the bread, when he carried out his fellowship at table with them even after the cross. As a result of that recognition, they hurried to the disciples in Jerusalem to share the good news, to tell the amazing story. Just so, the holy communion sends the communicants on their way rejoicing. Unless our celebrations are marked with that kind of joy, we have missed the point. Sometimes Christians approach the altar in such a somber mood that they belie the happy story they are supposedly enacting. The feast of eating and drinking with Jesus aims to produce real joy, the joy of healed and forgiven ones, dancing and shouting. After all, it is a story of resurrected life that is being enacted!

But That's Blasphemy—Unless

The point of all this can hardly be missed. If the church's life and work is marked by praying the Abba-prayer, by baptizing and absolving and communing, then everything that the church does which marks it as the church is blasphemy—its share in the blasphemy of Jesus. The church is the church as it acts out all of the things for which Jesus was charged with blasphemy. The church's churchliness consists of its perpetuation of those blasphemies. It insults God when we sinners make bold to use the family nickname, Abba. It insults God's reputation when as sinners we further dare to link our own forgiving with that which we claim from Abba. It is blasphemy to claim the right to adopt more sinners into the family by baptizing them and asserting that they, too, have a claim on the family inheritance of the forgiveness of sins. It is an insult to the God who alone has the right to forgive when and whom God chooses to forgive, when the church exercises the right given to it by Jesus when he commissioned his followers to forgive as he had forgiven. And it is pure blasphemy when we sinners, acknowledging our abject sinnerhood, nevertheless claim to have a place at the banquet table of the kingdom of God by linking our fame and fate with that of Jesus. That is all blasphemy, to be sure.

Unless the story of Jesus is the surprising truth about God. Unless Jesus, the friend of sinners, is the beloved Son whom God raised up and made to be both Lord and Christ. Unless, indeed, this Jesus, who was crucified as a blasphemer, spoke true and trustworthy promises when he offered forgiveness and newness of life to all sorts and conditions of sinners, and to the likes of us. Unless, of course, Jesus is Lord, and the mercy of God is the last word— also for us in our time. . . . And amazingly enough, the church is the community of befriended sinners who count on it!